MW01146230

Preparing for Eternity

Do We Trust God's Word or Religious Traditions?

By
Mike Gendron

PTG Publishing
2829 Veranda Lane
Southlake, TX 76092
www.ProclaimingTheGospel.org

PTG Publishing
2829 Veranda Lane, Southlake, TX 76092
www.ProclaimingTheGospel.org

Preparing for Eternity is © 2011 by Mike Gendron
ISBN 978-0-615-92124-2

Proclaiming the Gospel Ministry
2829 Veranda Lane
Southlake, TX 76092

Library of Congress Cataloging-in-Publication Data
Gendron, Mike.
  [Preparing Catholics for eternity]
  Preparing for eternity : Do we trust God's Word or religious traditions? / by Mike Gendron.
    p. cm.
  Originally published as: Preparing Catholics for eternity.
  ISBN 978-0-615-92124-2 (alk. paper)
  1. Salvation--Catholic Church. 2. Salvation--Biblical teaching. 3. Christian life--Catholic authors. 4. Christian life--Biblical teaching. 5. Catholic Church--Doctrines. I. Title.
  BT755.G46 2011
  234--dc23
                    2011024695

"Carefully and convincingly, this helpful book demonstrates that the 'gospel' taught in Roman Catholicism is not the true gospel found in the Bible. I heartily recommend Mike Gendron's work in these pages, as well as his continued ministry through Proclaiming the Gospel."

Dr. John MacArthur
Pastor/Teacher
Grace Community Church

"Mike Gendron has a message that is unique in its courage as well as its insight. He will challenge your mind and encourage your heart."

Dr. Paige Patterson
President
Southwestern Baptist Theo. Seminary

"Mike Gendron loves people. He has devoted his life to helping Catholics understand and embrace the true gospel of Jesus Christ. And he loves God's Word. He studies and teaches it with diligence and an unwavering commitment to its absolute authority. You will discover those qualities on every page of Two Ways to Eternity."

Tom Pennington
Senior Pastor
Countryside Bible Church

"Mike Gendron presents penetrating insights into Catholicism based both upon experience and biblical study with a spirit of love. His motivation is not to condemn, but to provide deliverance from faith in a religious system to faith in Jesus."

Dr. David Reagan
Evangelist
Lamb and Lion Ministries

Acknowledgments

This book has been made possible through the gracious generosity of the supporters of the Proclaiming the Gospel Ministry, along with their passion for the truth and their compassion for the lost.

www.ProclaimingTheGospel.org

Contents

PART 3:
An Eternity With Christ

PART 4: Equipping the Saints

Appendix 1

Appendix 2

Dedication

To all the precious souls in the Roman Catholic Church who may be where I was for most of my life, believing I was on my way to heaven but, according to the Bible, destined for an eternity without Christ.

It is my prayer that Catholics will test every man's teaching with the supreme authority of God's holy word. It is the most trustworthy authority for discerning truth from error.

May those who have been misled by the unbiblical traditions of men, forsake all efforts to save themselves, and come to Jesus with empty hands of faith, bringing nothing but their sins. He is the all-sufficient Savior who saves completely and forever.

May God be glorified as He reveals Himself to those who seek the truth through His Word.

About the Author

For 34 years Evangelist Mike Gendron was a devout Roman Catholic and a strong defender of what he believed to be the "one true church." However, in 1981, while attending an evangelical seminar, he heard for the first time that eternal life is not merited by good works, but is given freely by God's grace to those who put their faith and trust in the Lord Jesus Christ as their all-sufficient Savior. During the seminar, undeniable, objective truths were presented to establish the Bible as his final authority in all matters of faith. His new excitement and hunger for the inspired Word of God lead him to help organize the very first Little Rock Scripture Study in Dallas, Texas at St. Patrick's Catholic Church.

Mike soon realized many of the teachings and traditions of the Catholic Church were not found in the Bible. More importantly he was shocked to learn that the Roman Catholic plan of salvation was diametrically opposed to the biblical plan of salvation. After more study he discovered that those who believe and embrace the sacramental plan of salvation offered by the Vatican have only a false hope and remain spiritually dead in their sins.

No longer able to worship in a church that was taking its people down the wide road to destruction, Mike left the Catholic

Church in 1984 for a church where the true gospel is proclaimed and the Scriptures are the final authority in all matters of faith.

In 1988 he walked away from a successful career in corporate management to study at Dallas Theological Seminary (D.T.S.). During his studies Mike began to realize that his experience as a Roman Catholic was similar to the experiences of most other Catholics. He was taught from a very early age to trust and rely on the church, its priests, the sacraments, and his own good works for salvation. In 1991, during his last year at D.T.S., Mike's love for Catholics in-spired him to begin a ministry that would point Catholics to the Lord Jesus Christ and His perfect, complete, and finished work of salvation. His heart is now burdened for those who may be where he was for most of his life—eternally condemned and not even aware of it.

Introduction

The Lord Jesus declared that there are two ways to eternity—a narrow way that leads to life and a broad way that leads to destruction (Matthew 7:13–14). In the context of these verses we see our Lord warning people of false teachers who would try to lead people away from the narrow way. His warning has gone unheeded for 2,000 years. As a result of this widespread deception, very few ever find the narrow way. Tragically, there are many on the broad way, headed for everlasting torment. "There is a way that seems right unto man, but its end is the way of death" (Proverbs 14:12). The most important issue we all face in this life is determining which is the true way to spending eternity with God in His favorable presence. Our Creator answered that question with clarity and assurance when He declared, "I am the way…no one comes to the Father except through Me" (John 14:6). Those who hear His Word and follow Him in faith are "the few" who have found the narrow way.

In this book I have presented the Word of God as the eternal truth that exposes every false way. It is my hope that readers will recognize God's Word for what it is—the supreme authority for all matters of faith. It is the authority that must judge every religious teaching and tradition. This book you now hold in your hands has been a labor of love because of my great love and deep compassion for people who are more loyal to a religion than to the Lord Jesus Christ. It is an objective look at the teaching of a religion through the lens of Holy Scripture. Readers will recognize that it is impossible to believe many Roman Catholic traditions and the Word of God at the same time. They are diametrically opposed.

Opposing views of theology cannot be reconciled unless one of them changes. Roman Catholicism, whose very motto is "semper idem," or "always the same," cannot change. The Word of God is forever settled in heaven and therefore can never change. And, since they are different theologies, they cannot both be right.

It is my heart's desire that the reader will take what is written and examine it according to God's Word. I have not given my opinions about Roman teachings, but have cited the official authorities of the Roman Catholic Church. May God use this book, which is filled with His Word, to reach some who are willing to look rationally and objectively at what they believe and what they have been taught. The subject of where people will spend eternity is a most serious subject to investigate. To God be all glory, honor, and praise!

Mike Gendron
Southlake, Texas

Part I

Work Out Your Salvation With Fear and Trembling

1

The Most Trustworthy Authority

The most important decision any of us makes in this life is choosing which authority to trust for our eternal destiny. We can be wrong about a lot of things in this life and still survive, but if we are wrong about which authority to trust for life after death we will pay for that mistake for all eternity. Every religion has an authority. It may be a person, a book, an experience, or a combination of all three. But is there one authority that is more trustworthy than all others? Is there a supreme authority that has no equal? The Catholic Church recognizes the Bible as a sacred book, but not as the sole and final authority for truth. Regardless, there is no equal to the Bible, for it is the most authoritative, influential, and powerful book ever written.

God chose forty men to pen His Word as they were carried along by the Holy Spirit (2 Peter 1:21). The writers claim they were transmitting the very Word of God, infallible and authoritative to the highest degree. Since it is impossible for God to lie, His Word must be the standard by which we discern truth from error (Hebrews 6:18; 1 John 4:6). God has exalted His Word above all things. He has even made it equal to His holy name (Psalm 138:2). Jesus used the power and authority of the Scriptures to rebuke Satan (Matthew 4). God's Word is sufficient to function as the sole infallible rule of faith. The Bible does not refer to any other rule of faith because everything that one must know, understand, and believe to become a Christian is found in the Scriptures (2 Timothy 3:14-16; 1 Corinthians 15:1–4). Therefore, after considering each source of authority, we must ask, "But what does the Scripture say" (Galatians 4:30)? We must also heed Paul's exhortation: "Do not go beyond what is written" (1 Corinthians 4:6). What is your authority for truth? Is it absolutely trustworthy? Has it ever been wrong before? Is it possible for it ever to mislead or deceive you? There can be only one answer!

The Bible's supreme authority is established by its divine origin. God has spoken to us through the Scriptures. The Bible is the only book that can claim all of the following characteristics:

Prophecy–It foretells the future with great precision and detail.

Influence–There is abundant evidence of radically changed lives throughout human history.

Unity–All books fit together to describe one complex drama from eternity to eternity.

Indestructibility–It has withstood continuous attacks and intense scrutiny.

God Inspired–The Bible is the only religious book that gives solid proof of its divine inspiration.

Freedom–The Bible is the only book that has power to set people free from bondage.

Popularity–It is the most circulated and translated book in history (1800 languages).

Character–The Bible was written by 40 authors from all walks of life, spanning 1500 years and 3 continents.

Reliability–All its historical, geographical, and cultural references agree with external contemporary evidence.

In any study about God and His plan for the human race, a major issue that needs to be dealt with is authority. In whom or what will you place your trust? The decision usually boils down to trusting the Lord Jesus Christ and His Word or the teachings and traditions of men.

Consequently, faith comes from hearing the message, and the message is heard through the word of Christ (Romans 10:17).

The Bible is the most unique book ever written. No other religious book dares to predict the future. When the Bible was written, over 30% of the Scriptures foretold of future prophetic events. We have seen over half of these prophecies fulfilled in the precise time and manner as predicted in the Scriptures. There are extensive prophecies dealing with nations and cities, all of which have been literally fulfilled. Jesus Christ fulfilled three hundred prophecies at His first coming, and many more will be fulfilled at His Second Coming. Only a book inspired by God, who alone knows the end from the beginning, could foretell the future with 100% accuracy. See if you can find seven characteristics of the Bible from these verses.

All your words are true (Psalm 119:160).

....from infancy you have known the Holy Scriptures, which are able to make you wise for salvation through faith in Christ Jesus. All Scripture is God-breathed and is useful for teaching, rebuking, correcting and training in righteousness, (2 Timothy 3:15–16).

For the Word of God is living and active. Sharper than any double-edged sword, it penetrates even to dividing soul and spirit, joints and marrow; it judges the thoughts and attitudes of the heart (Hebrews 4:12).

We have the word of the prophets made more certain, and you will do well to pay attention to it, as to a light shining in a dark place, until the day dawns and the morning star rises in your hearts. For prophecy never had its origin in the will of man, but men spoke from God as they were carried along by the Holy Spirit (2 Peter 1:19–21).

The Apostle Paul commended the Berean Church for using Scriptures to verify the truthfulness of his teaching. Since an apostle, who wrote over fifty percent of the New Testament, was tested by Scripture, should not all religious leaders come under the same type of scrutiny? Have you checked the teachings of your religious leaders with the Bible? What was the Bereans' authority?

Now the Bereans were of more noble character than the Thessalonians, for they received the message with great eager-ness and examined the Scriptures every day to see if what Paul said was true (Acts 17:11).

The Catechism of the Catholic Church (CCC) states, "The task of giving an authentic interpretation of the Word of God has been entrusted to the living teaching office (the Magisterium) of the Church alone" (para. 85). All Catholics are required to comply with all the teachings of their Magisterium (para. 88). "To check unbridled spirits, it decrees that no one relying on his own judgment shall....in accordance with his own conceptions, presume to interpret them (Scriptures) contrary to holy mother Church... Those who act contrary to this shall be made known by the ordinaries and punished in accordance with the penalties prescribed by the law" (Decree Concerning Use of the Sacred Books, Council Of Trent, Fourth Session). Catholics are asked to trust a group of fallible men to interpret the Word of God for them.

Were the Scriptures given to a select group of men (Magisterium) to interpret or to every man?

Rather, we have renounced secret and shameful ways; we do not use deception, nor do we distort the word of God. On the con-

trary, by setting forth the truth plainly we commend our-selves to every man's conscience in the sight of God (2 Corinthians 4:2).

The Catholic Church teaches that Peter was the chief apostle and the rock upon which Jesus would build His church. They base this doctrine on a misinterpretation of Matthew 16:18 where Jesus said, "You are Peter (petros–stone) and on this rock (petra–mass of rock) I will build my church." However, the Greek word "petra" is feminine, and therefore it is not normal to use it in reference to the masculine Peter. Jesus did not say, "upon thee I will build my church." Peter knew without a doubt that Jesus was not referring to him as "the rock," because he proclaimed Jesus as "the rock" (1 Peter 2:6–8). "Petra" must refer to Peter's confession of faith that he made after Jesus asked him, "Who do you say I am." Paul also referred to Jesus as the rock: "They drank from the spiritual rock that accompanied them, and that rock was Christ" (1 Corinthians 10:4). It was James, not Peter, who presided over the Jerusalem Council (Acts 15:13, 19). And it was the apostles who sent Peter to preach, rather than Peter sending them (Acts 8:14). Who is the foundation, the chief cornerstone, and the head of the church?

> *For no one can lay any foundation other than the one al-ready laid, which is Jesus Christ (1 Corinthians 3:11).*

> *And God placed all things under His (Christ's) feet and ap-pointed Him to be head over everything for the church, which is His body, the fullness of Him who fills everything in every way. (The church or household of God is) built on the foun-dation of the apostles and prophets, with Christ Jesus himself as the chief cornerstone (Ephesians 1:22–23; 2:20).*

The Catholic Church teaches that Jesus gave Peter and his successors authority over the church when He offered them the keys to the kingdom (Matthew 16:19). Peter first opened heaven by proclaiming the gospel to the Jews (Acts 2:14), then the Gentiles (Acts 15:7, 14). It is only by believing the gospel that people are loosed from their sins. Anyone who rejects the gospel remains bound in his or her sin. All born-again Christians possess these keys. The gospel is clearly the only key that can open the gates of heaven.

I am not ashamed of the gospel, because it is the power of God for the salvation of everyone who believes: first for the Jew, then for the Gentile (Romans 1:16).

Whoever believes in the Son has eternal life, but whoever rejects the Son will not see life, for God's wrath remains on him (John 3:36).

The Catholic Church declares its popes are infallible when speaking "ex cathedra," or "from the authority of their office" in matters of faith and morals, but are they really? There have been numerous accounts of popes contradicting each other's proclamations as well as the Bible. When we look at the life of Peter, whom Catholics believe was their first pope, we see clearly that he was not infallible. Paul used the gospel to show Peter he was wrong in Galatians 2:11–14.

When Peter came to Antioch, I opposed him to his face, be-cause he was clearly in the wrong. . . . The other Jews joined him in his hypocrisy, so that by their hypocrisy even Barnabas was led astray. When I saw that they were not acting in line with the truth of the Gospel, I said to Peter in front of them all, "You are a Jew, yet you live like a Gentile and not like a Jew. How is it, then, that you force Gentiles to follow Jewish customs" (Galatians 2:11–14)?

Jesus turned and said to Peter, "Get behind me, Satan! You are a stumbling block to me; you do not have in mind the things of God, but the things of men" (Matthew 16:23).

Peter asked, "Lord, why can't I follow you now? I will lay down my life for you." Then Jesus answered, "Will you really lay down your life for me? I tell you the truth, before the rooster crows, you will disown me three times" (John 13:37–38).

Jesus never established the papacy or a hierarchy of authority for the church. In fact, He instructed the apostles to avoid ruling the church this way.

Jesus said, "You know that the rulers of the Gentiles lord it over them, and their high officials exercise authority over them. Not so with you. Instead, whoever wants to become great among you must be your servant (Matthew 20:25–26).

Yet today we see within the Roman Catholic Church an enormous structure of monsignors, bishops, archbishops, cardinals, and a pope ruling over the lay people. What did Jesus say would be the characteristic of greatness? What warnings do the Sacred Scriptures give to those who trust the teachings of men rather than God and His Word?

This is what the Lord says: "Cursed is the one who trusts in man, who depends on flesh for his strength and whose heart turns away from the Lord. He will be like a bush in the wastelands....But blessed is the man who trusts in the Lord, whose confidence is in Him" (Jeremiah 17:5–7).

It is better to take refuge in the Lord than to trust in man (Psalm 118:8).

This is the fate of those who trust in themselves, and of their followers, who approve their sayings, like sheep they are des-tined for the grave and death will feed on them (Psalm 49:13–14).

Do not put your trust in princes, in mortal men, who cannot save. When their spirit departs, they return to the ground; on that very day their plans come to nothing. Blessed is he whose help is the God of Jacob, whose hope is in the Lord his God (Psalm 146:3–5).

The Roman Catholic Church teaches that Scripture and tradition must be accepted and honored with equal sentiments of devotion, reverence, and authority (CCC, para. 82 and 95). This has led to numerous traditions that oppose or nullify the gospel. God's Word has no equal when it comes to authority. It is pure, perfect, inerrant, infallible, living, sure, truth, light, holy, eternal, forever settled in heaven, and will exist even if heaven and earth pass away. It illuminates, cleanses, saves, frees, guides, converts, heals, quickens, judges, and sanctifies. It also brings conviction, gives knowledge, gives wisdom, produces faith, refutes error, searches the heart, equips for every good work, and is used as a weapon. Few, if any, of these characteristics can be said about Catholic tradition. What is the proper relationship between tradition and Scripture?

Jesus, said, "They worship me in vain; their teachings are but rules taught by men. You have let go of the commands of God and are holding on to the traditions of men. Thus you nullify the word of God by your tradition that you have handed down. And you do many things like that" (Mark 7:7–8, 13).

See to it that no one takes you captive through hollow and deceptive philosophy, which depends on human tradition and the basic principles of this world rather than on Christ (Colossians 2:8).

The Roman Catholic Church teaches that the Bible is not a sufficient rule of faith, but that God's revelation is also contained in Tradition. To support this idea they cite John 21:25: "Jesus did many other things as well. If every one of them were written down, I suppose that even the whole world would not have room for the books that would be written." Most Roman Catholic traditions have been developed since the apostles' teaching, such as Mary's immaculate conception and assumption into heaven, papal infallibility, purgatory, and indulgences. Since none of these are apostolic traditions taught in the first century they are to be rejected because they oppose God's Word. Note the tense of the verbs given in the following verses:

So then, brethren, stand firm and hold to the traditions which you were taught, whether by word of mouth or by letter from us (2 Thessalonians 2:15).

Dear friends, although I was very eager to write to you about the salvation we share, I felt I had to write and urge you to contend for the faith that was once for all entrusted to the saints (Jude 3).

The Catholic Church establishes its universal authority by pro-nouncing itself the "one true church" and declares "outside the church there is no salvation" (CCC, para. 846). How does God's Word define "the true church"?

> *To the church of God in Corinth, to those sanctified in Christ Jesus and called to be holy, together with all those everywhere who call on the name of our Lord Jesus Christ (1 Corinthians 1:2).*

> *To the church of the firstborn, whose names are written in heaven. You have come to God, the judge of all men, to the spirits of righteous men made perfect (Hebrews 12:23).*

What will happen to those who supplant God's authority by adding to His Word?

> *Every word of God is flawless; He is a shield to those who take refuge in Him. Do not add to His words, or He will re-buke you and prove you a liar (Proverbs 30:5–6).*

The Roman Catholic Church has added to the Word of God. The Catholic Bible contains not only the 39 books of the Old Testa-ment and the 27 books of the New Testa-ment, but also the apoc-ryphal books, Tobit, Judith, Wisdom, Ecclesiasticus, Baruch and Maccabees. These books were never part of the early church canon because they contain historical and geographical errors, proving that they were not divinely inspired. The apocryphal books also teach doctrines that are at variance with the inspired Scriptures. For example, 2 Maccabees 12:43–45 teaches the efficacy of prayers and offerings for the dead. Ecclesiasticus 3:30 teaches that alms-giving makes atonement for sin and justifies cruelty to slaves (33:26, 28). Christ and His apostles quoted frequently from Old Testament books, but never from these apocryphal books. Furthermore, they were never included in the Jewish canon, which is of utmost signif-icance. To whom did God entrust His Word?

> *(The Jews) were entrusted with the oracles of God (Romans 3:1–2).*

The Roman Catholic Church has removed portions of God's Word from its Catechisms. In the new Catechism of the Catholic Church, the second commandment of God has been removed. The Vatican also divided the tenth commandment into two to replace the one they removed. What Catholic practice is in violation of the second commandment?

> *You shall not make for yourself an idol, or any likeness of what is in heaven above or on the earth beneath or in the waters under the earth (Exodus 20:4).*

By deleting the second commandment from their catechism, what command has the Catholic Church broken?

> *Do not add to what I command you and do not subtract from it, but keep the commands of the Lord your God that I give you. (Deuteronomy 4:2).*

Roman Catholics contend that the Catholic Church gave birth to the Bible, established the canon at the Council of Hippo in A.D. 393, and therefore is the only infallible interpreter of Scripture. However history reveals a different story on the development of the canon. Long before a church council formally recognized the canon, the books were received and recognized as being the inspired Word of God. They were functioning with supreme and complete authority in matters of faith and doctrine. To separate the inspired writings from other spurious writings and place them into one volume was the task given to Christians who were already converted to Christ through the Word (1 Peter 1:23). Therefore it was the Bible that gave birth to the church, not the church that gave birth to the Bible. The canon was determined by God and discovered by man. What proof do we have that letters were circulated and accepted before the canon was formally established?

> *After this letter has been read to you, see that it is also read in the church of the Laodiceans (Colossians 4:16).*

Roman Catholics argue that the reason there are over 25,000 Protestant denominations is because there is no infallible Protestant interpreter to teach the Bible correctly. They contend that there is no unity, only divisions, among the churches and denominations that submit to "Sola Scriptura." We need to correct this misunderstanding with the truth. The denominations that submit to "Sola Scriptura" are much more unified than religious institutions and cults that submit to the "Bible plus an infallible interpreter." Mormons and Catholics, who both use the "Bible plus an infallible interpreter" system, do not refer to one another as brothers-in-Christ, but exclude one another as heretics. On the other hand, most denominations in the "Sola Scriptura" camp would definitely refer to one another as brothers. In fact, if we were to randomly select five denominations that submit to "Sola Scriptura" and compare them with five that submit to the "Bible plus an infallible interpreter" as the rule of faith, the former group would be much more unified than the latter. True unity is found whenever it is centered on the true gospel.

Roman Catholics claim that if anyone studies church history and the early church it will lead them to the "one true church" of Rome. However, for anyone to rely on their own interpretation to come to any such conclusion goes against the very teaching of Roman Catholicism. According to Rome, we cannot trust our own ability to understand and interpret Matthew 16:18 and church history. So, if this is true, how can anyone be sure that God's infallible interpreter is Roman Catholicism? In other words, how can a Catholic know his religion is infallible when he must rely on his fallible interpretation to arrive at that conclusion? Every "infallible interpreter" claims you cannot understand Scripture and church history without their help. Eastern Orthodox, Mormons, and Jehovah's Witnesses all make the same claim. Therefore, if we were to choose one of the "infallible interpreters" over the others, how can we possibly know we have made the right choice? Furthermore, if we make the wrong choice, we risk eternal damnation for trusting an "infallible" interpreter rather than our own judgment of what the infallible Word of God says.

Some Catholics may argue that their religion does not forbid private interpretation of Scripture. However, when the truth of God's Word began setting thousands of people free from the bondage of religious deception, Rome tried to prevent access to the truth. The 16th century Council of Trent gathered the Bishops of the Catholic Church together to counter the Protestant Reformation. The Bishops not only placed the Bible on the list of forbidden books, but also outlawed private interpretation of Scriptures. From the 4th Session of the Council we read: "In order to restrain petulant spirits, it decrees that no one, relying on his own skill, shall, in matters of faith, and of morals pertaining to the edification of Christian doctrine, wresting the sacred Scripture to his own senses, presume to interpret the said sacred Scripture contrary to that sense which holy mother Church, whose it is to judge of the true sense and interpretation of the holy Scriptures." The Second Vatican Council restated the dogma this way: "The task of authentically interpreting the word of God, whether written or handed on, has been entrusted exclusively to the living teaching office of the Church." The Council went on to pronounce: "The way of interpreting Scripture is subject finally to the judgment of the Church, which carries out the divine commission and ministry of guarding and interpreting the word of God" (Dei Verbum, II, 10 and III, 12).

The Apostle Paul, who wrote more than half the New Testament, understood Scripture to be the final and supreme authority in matters of faith. In his letter to the churches of Galatia, he encouraged every believer to use private judgment in discerning truth from error. He warned readers not to believe anyone who comes preaching a gospel that is different from the one already delivered by the apostles (Galatians 1:6–9). Since the original gospel is completely contained in Scripture, it must be every Christian's standard for making private judgments (1 Corinthians 15:1–4). Paul included himself and even angels from heaven as "religious authorities" that must be tested for veracity. Every man's teaching, whether it comes from popes, bishops, pastors, evangelists or faith healers, must conform to the written Word of God. If it does not conform it must be rejected. We know that the books of the New Testament were not addressed to bishops but, in most cases, to individual saints. Paul said, "by the manifestation of truth we commend ourselves to every man's conscience in the sight of God" (2 Corinthians 4:2). If we take Paul seriously, we will engage in private judgment and interpretation of God's Word to test the authenticity of any religious teachers (Acts 17:11). Those who do not heed his exhortation risk the fatal mistake of following false teachers and turning from Jesus.

We must become serious students of the Bible to avoid being deceived by religious teachers. In doing so, we need to follow some important principles of interpretation. Always approach the study of God's Word with a teachable spirit and a desire to be taught by the Holy Spirit, our most trustworthy teacher (1 John 2:27). We must interpret passages literally unless they were written in a figurative or allegorical sense. It is important to observe the context for each verse and seek to understand the writer's intent and the historical and cultural setting in which the events took place. It is always wise to compare Scripture with Scripture and interpret each passage consistent with God's complete revelation. Difficult passages can be cleared up by comparing them with other passages that relate to the same subject. By studying word meanings and grammar carefully, and by consulting the original languages, we can gain a deeper understanding of a passage.

There is no higher authority than almighty God, who speaks only the truth and cannot lie (Titus 1:2). He inspired the Scriptures to reveal Himself to mankind through Jesus Christ as Creator, Lord, and Savior. Jesus Christ is the personification of truth, and His Word is truth (John 14:6; 17:17). Why would anyone choose to look anywhere else for truth? Scripture must be the supreme and infallible authority in all that it reveals. We know that God does not try to confuse anyone about life's most critical issue—"What must I do to be saved?" However, to avoid being confused or deceived by religious teachers, we must put away any Catholic or Protestant tradition or teaching that opposes His inspired authoritative Word!

What caution would you give to anyone who uses the "early church fathers" as an authority over the Word of God?

> *I know that after I leave, savage wolves will come in among you and will not spare the flock. Even from your own number men will arise and distort the truth in order to draw away disciples after them. So be on your guard! Remember that for three years I never stopped warning each of you night and day with tears (Acts 20:29–31).*

2

Knowledge of the Truth

Knowledge of the truth about God is foundational and essential for genuine conversion. God wants men to be saved and to come to a knowledge of the truth (1 Timothy 2:4). So our prayer should be like that of King David: "Show me your ways, O Lord, teach me your paths; guide me in your truth and teach me, for you are God my Savior, and my hope is in you all day long" (Psalm 25:4–5). But where can we go to learn the truth about God and His plan of redemption? Is the Bible sufficient, or do we need other sources for this truth? With so many religious beliefs in the world today, how can we discern God's truth from the error of some religious leaders? These are critical questions that are answered by the personification of truth—the Lord Jesus Christ. Those who have been deceived by religious leaders will never know it unless they are confronted with the truth.

The Scriptures reveal that Jesus is the truth, His Word is truth, and He came to testify to the truth. Those who follow the Lord Jesus and His Word can discern truth from error.

> *Jesus answered, "I am the way and the truth and the life. No one comes to the Father except through me" (John 14:6).*
>
> *Sanctify them by the truth; your word is truth (John 17:17).*

> *Jesus said, "For this reason I was born, and for this I came into the world, to testify to the truth everyone on the side of truth listens to me" (John 18:37).*
>
> *And you also were included in Christ when you heard the word of truth, the gospel of your salvation. Having believed, you were marked in Him with a seal, the promised Holy Spirit (Ephesians 1:13).*
>
> *Jesus replied, "You are in error because you do not know the Scriptures or the power of God" (Matthew 22:29).*

What is the role and the ministry of the Holy Spirit in regard to truth?

> *But when He, the Spirit of truth, comes, He will guide you into all truth (John 16:13).*
>
> *I am writing these things to you about those who are trying to lead you astray. As for you, the anointing you received from Him (the Holy Spirit) remains in you, and you do not need anyone to teach you (1 John 2:26–27).*
>
> *And it is the Spirit who testifies, because the Spirit is the truth (1 John 5:6).*

Jesus said, "If you hold to my teaching, you are really my disciples. Then you will know the truth, and the truth will set you free" (John 8:31–32). If you know the truth, what will it set you free from?

> *See to it that no one takes you captive through hollow and deceptive philosophy, which depends on human tradition and the basic principles of this world rather than on Christ (Colossians 2:8).*
>
> *This matter arose because some false brothers had infiltrated our ranks to spy on the freedom we have in Christ Jesus and to make us slaves (Galatians 2:4).*
>
> *Those who oppose him he must gently instruct, in the hope that*

God will grant them repentance leading them to a knowledge of the truth, and that they will come to their senses and escape from the trap of the devil, who has taken them captive to do his will (2 Timothy 2:25–26).

At one time we too were foolish, disobedient, deceived and enslaved by all kinds of passions and pleasures. We lived in malice and envy, being hated and hating one another (Titus 3:3).

What consequences await those who neglect or reject God's truth?

But for those who are self-seeking and who reject the truth and follow evil, there will be wrath and anger (Romans 2:8).

They perish because they refused to love the truth and so be saved (2 Thessalonians 2:10).

…all will be condemned who have not believed the truth but have delighted in wickedness (2 Thessalonians 2:12).

Just as Jannes and Jambres opposed Moses, so also these men oppose the truth, men of depraved minds, who, as far as the faith is concerned, are rejected (2 Timothy 3:8).

My people are destroyed from lack of knowledge (Hosea 4:6).

What do men worship and serve when they reject God's truth and accept a lie?

They exchanged the truth of God for a lie, and worshipped and served created things rather than the Creator—who is forever praised (Romans 1:25).

What kind of worshippers does God seek?

God is Spirit, and His worshippers must worship in spirit and in truth (John 4:24).

Anyone who worships God in a church that distorts or withholds the truth of the Bible is encouraged to find a church with biblical integrity.

> *I know that after I leave, savage wolves will come in among you and will not spare the flock. Even from your own number men will arise and distort the truth in order to draw away disciples after them. So be on your guard! Remember that for three years I never stopped warning each of you night and day with tears (Acts 20:29–31).*

If we love someone who is deceived, should we lovingly confront him or her with the truth or let them live in deception?

> *Love does not delight in evil but rejoices with the truth (1 Corinthians 13:6).*

> *For we cannot do anything against the truth, but only for the truth (2 Corinthians 13:8).*

> *We did not give in to them for a moment, so that the truth of the gospel might remain with you (Galatians 2:5).*

> *Stand firm then, with the belt of truth buckled around your waist (Ephesians 6:14).*

How can we know the true faith of the apostles? How do we know the true faith was signed, sealed, and delivered to the 1st century saints?

> *And for this purpose I (Paul) was appointed a herald and an apostle—I am telling the truth, I am not lying—and a teacher of the true faith to the Gentiles (1 Timothy 2:7).*

> *Paul, a servant of God and an apostle of Jesus Christ for the faith of God's elect and the knowledge of the truth that leads to godliness (Titus 1:1).*

> *Dear friends, although I was very eager to write to you about the salvation we share, I felt I had to write and*

urge you to contend for the faith that was once for all entrusted to the saints (Jude 3).

Knowledge of the truth will bring division. Those who follow Jesus by abiding in His Word will be divided from those who do not.

Jesus said, "Do you suppose that I came to grant peace on earth? I tell you, no, but rather division; for from now on five members in one household will be divided...They will be divided, father against son, and son against father; mother against daughter, and daughter against mother" (Luke 12:51–53).

Doctrine divides believers from unbelievers. Without doctrine there will be no division.

Know Doctrine —Know Division
No Doctrine —No Division

3

Salvation Proclaimed in the Gospel

Jesus saves everyone who obeys the first command of His earthly ministry: "Repent and believe the gospel" (Mark 1:15). He saves them from the penalty and power of sin. Eternal life is given as a gift of God's grace and mercy to sinners who deserve condemnation. Without possession of this wonderful gift, man is eternally separated from God and will suffer everlasting punishment (2 Thessalonians 1:8). Our almighty and sovereign God is holy and righteous and must punish sin (Habakkuk 1:12–13; Exodus 34:6, 7). Everyone who is born in this world is conceived in sin, is born a sinner, and comes under the judgment of God (Romans 3:10, 23). The penalty for sin is death (Romans 6:23), and the second death is the eternal lake of fire (Revelation 20:14). But God did not leave everyone dead in their sins (Ephesians 2:1). For those who believe, God demonstrated His love for them in that while they were sinners Christ died for them (Romans 5:8). Eternal life is free because the Lord Jesus Christ paid the ransom for our redemption with His shed blood (Titus 2:13–14). Jesus, the sinless Savior, suffered the wrath of God, paying the death penalty that God demands of sinners (2 Corinthians 5:21). We can be reconciled to God only through Jesus Christ, His only Son (John 14:6). Faith appropriates the work accomplished by Christ.

Jesus lived a perfectly righteous life by obeying and fulfilling the law of God (Hebrews 7:26; Colossians 2:14). Since perfect righteousness is necessary to enter heaven (Revelation 21:27), and since it is impossible for sinners to become righteous, God offers us the righteousness of His Son as a gift to those who come to Him with empty hands of faith (Romans 5:17). God justifies the wicked when they put their faith in the only righteous one— Jesus Christ (Romans 4:5). Everyone God justifies, He ultimately glorifies (Romans 8:30). The gift of eternal life can only be received by repentance (Acts 3:19) and faith (John 3:36). This gift is eternally secure because God's gifts are irrevocable (Romans 11:29). Salvation can only be received by grace, God's unmerited favor (Ephesians 2:8–9). It cannot be merited by righteous deeds because anyone who works to earn acceptance before God nullifies the grace of God (Titus 3:5; Romans 11:6). Those who receive Jesus Christ by grace through faith are adopted into God's eternal family and nothing can ever separate them from God's love (John 1:12; Romans 8:38–39). Jesus Christ loses no one that the Father gives Him because they rest in the palm of His hand (John 6:39; 10:27–30).

What response to the gospel does God require of sinners who desire eternal life?

> *Whoever believes in the Son has eternal life, but whoever rejects the Son will not see life, for God's wrath remains on him (John 3:36).*

> *I tell you the truth, whoever hears my word and believes Him who sent me has eternal life and will not be condemned; he has crossed over from death to life (John 5:24).*

To believe the Lord Jesus Christ is to believe He is fully God and fully man, and to believe His atoning sacrifice was necessary and sufficient to appease the wrath of God for sin. Anyone who repents and receives Jesus Christ as Lord and Savior by grace through faith in His life, death, and resurrection, ceasing to trust in anything else for salvation, becomes a child of God and receives the gift of eternal life, which can never be revoked. To believe in Jesus is to believe His gospel. Is the gospel according to Scripture or Tradition?

> *Now, brothers, I want to remind you of the gospel I preached to you, which you received and on which you have taken your stand. By this gospel you are saved, if you hold firmly to the word I preached to you. Otherwise, you have believed in vain. For what I received I passed on to you as of first importance: that Christ died for our sins according to the Scriptures, that he was buried, that he was raised on the third day according to the Scriptures (1 Corinthians 15:1–4).*

> *I am not ashamed of the gospel, because it is the power of God for the salvation of everyone who believes: first for the Jew, then for the Gentile. For in the gospel a righteousness from God is revealed, a righteousness that is by faith from first to last, just as it is written: "The righteous will live by faith" (Romans 1:16–17).*

The Apostle Paul preached that the gospel must remain pure and it must never be compromised (Galatians 2:5 and 1 Corinthians 15:2). What warning is given to anyone who dares to preach a different gospel?

> *I am astonished that you are so quickly deserting the one who called you by the grace of Christ and are turning to a different gospel, which is really no gospel at all. Evidently some people are throwing you into confusion and are trying to pervert the Gospel of Christ. But even if we or an angel from heaven should preach a gospel other than the one we preached to you, let him be eternally condemned! As we have already said, so now I say again: If anybody is preaching to you a gospel other than what you accepted, let him be eternally condemned (Galatians 1:6–9)!*

The Catholic Church preaches a different gospel by adding additional requirements for salvation. In addition to faith, Catholics must fulfill all the requirements of the Church, including water baptism, receiving the sacraments, attendance at Mass, church membership, and indulgences (CCC, para. 1256, 1129, 1405, 846, 1498). How are we to respond to those who preach a different gospel?

> *Rebuke them sharply, so that they will be sound in the faith and will pay no attention to Jewish myths or to the commands of those who reject the truth. To the pure, all things are pure, but to those who are corrupted and do not believe, nothing is pure. In fact, both their minds and consciences are corrupted. They claim to know God, but by their actions they deny him. They are detestable, disobedient and unfit for doing anything good (Titus 1:13–16).*

4

Forgiveness of Sin

Jesus Christ, the perfect High Priest offered Himself, the perfect sacrifice, to a perfect God, who demands perfection, then He cried out in victory, "It is finished" (John 19:30). The death of Jesus Christ provided forgiveness and expiation for all the sins of all who repent and believe His Gospel of grace. The forgiveness of sin is an act of God's justice that cancels the complete debt owed for sin. According to the Bible, only God can forgive sins. Jesus is the perfect and final sacrifice through which God's forgiveness is mediated to every believer. Jesus saw His own death as the fulfillment of the Old Testament sacrifices for sin. At the Last Supper He spoke of His death as "the New Covenant in my blood which is poured out for you" (Luke 22:20). Only the blood of Christ can purify sin. Jesus is the unblemished Sacrifice offered once, for all our sins, for all time. He saves completely those who come to God through Him (Hebrews 7:25). That means there is no residual sin to purge away in purgatory or residual punishment to be remitted by indulgences. The complete forgiveness of sins is available to those who trust Jesus Christ and His finished work on the cross. Yet Roman Catholicism denies these glorious truths of the Gospel.

What is the necessary substance for the forgiveness of sins?

> *This is my blood of the covenant, which is poured out for many for the forgiveness of sins (Matthew 26:28).*

> *In Him we have redemption through His blood, the for-*
> *giveness of sins, in accordance with the riches of God's grace*
> *(Ephesians 1:7).*
>
> *In fact, the law requires that nearly everything be cleansed*
> *with blood, and without the shedding of blood there is no*
> *for-giveness (Hebrews 9:22).*

The animal blood sacrifices of the Old Testament were a fore-shadowing of the blood sacrifice of Jesus. How were they different in their frequency and effect?

> *Once a year Aaron shall make atonement on its horns.*
> *This annual atonement must be made with the blood of*
> *the atoning sin offering for the generations to come. It is*
> *most holy to the Lord (Exodus 30:10).*

God presented Him as a sacrifice of atonement, through faith in his blood. He did this to demonstrate his justice, because in his forbearance He had left the sins committed beforehand unpunished (Romans 3:25).

What is necessary for a sinner's sins to be forgiven?

> *When Jesus saw their faith, he said, "Friend, your sins are*
> *forgiven" (Luke 5:20).*

> *…they may receive forgiveness of sins and a place among*
> *those who are sanctified by faith in me (Acts 26:18).*

The Roman Catholic Church teaches that infants are forgiven of original sin when a priest pours water over the baby in the sacrament of baptism. There are two serious problems with this practice. First, there is no occurrence of infant baptism in the New Testament and, second, one must believe in Jesus in order to be forgiven. Clearly a baby cannot respond in faith to the gospel and thus be forgiven.

All the prophets testify about Him that everyone who believes in Him receives forgiveness of sins through His name (Acts 10:43).

The Roman Catholic Church teaches two classifications of sin. A venial sin is a small offense against God that incurs only a temporal punishment, while a mortal sin is a serious offense against God that incurs an eternal punishment. The Bible teaches that all sins are mortal and are deserving of the eternal lake of fire. What is one guilty of for committing the smallest offense?

For whoever keeps the whole law and yet stumbles at just one point is guilty of breaking all of it (James 2:10).

The Catholic Church teaches that temporal punishment for venial sins can be expiated in this life through good works, prayer, sorrows, and last rites, or in the next life in Purgatory. "An indulgence is the remission before God of the temporal punishment due to sins and may be applied to the living or the dead" (CCC, para. 1471). How cruel it is to tell people that, even though God offers the complete forgiveness of their sins, they nevertheless must pay for them through acts of penance or by securing an indulgence from the church.

Early in the 16th century John Tetzel, a Dominican monk, claimed, "Indulgences are the most precious of God's gifts. Come and I will give you letters, all properly sealed by which even the sins that you intend to commit may be pardoned. There is no sin so great that an indulgence cannot remit; only pay well and all will be forgiven." Such teaching leaves people full of doubt and fear and at the mercy of their church. It devalues the work of Jesus Christ and robs Him of His glory and power. The Bible does not teach temporal punishment for sin.

For the wages of sin is death (Romans 6:23).

The lake of fire is the second death (Revelation 20:14).

> *He will punish those who do not know God and do not obey the gospel of our Lord Jesus. They will be punished with everlasting destruction and shut out from the presence of the Lord and from the majesty of his power (2 Thessalonians 1:8–9).*

> *Jesus will say, "Depart from me, you who are cursed, into the eternal fire prepared for the devil and his angels" (Matthew 25:41).*

Vatican Council II commands that the usage of indulgences should be kept in the Church and condemns with an anathema those who say that indulgences are useless or that the Church does not have the power to grant them (Sacred Liturgy, Chapter IV). In other words, the Vatican officially curses, or condemns to hell, those who deny the power or reality of indulgences. The Catholic Church teaches that indulgences "are distributed to the faithful for their salvation." The source of indulgences is the treasury of the Church where the merits and good works of the Blessed Virgin and of all the saints are known to add to the merits of Christ. "In this way Catholics attain their own salvation and at the same time cooperate in saving their brothers" (CCC, para.1477).

Can anything of value be added to the complete, perfect, and finished work of Christ on Calvary? Can anyone cooperate in saving themselves or others?

> *No man can redeem the life of another or give to God a ransom for him, the ransom for a life is costly, no payment is ever enough (Psalm 49:7–8).*

The Catholic Church teaches that Purgatory is a place where sinners incur a temporal punishment for venial sins and confessed mortal sins (CCC, para. 1030, 311 1472-75). Those in Purgatory remain there until the fire has purged their sins or until enough indulgences and masses have been appropriated for their release. Can fire purge or cleanse anyone of sin? Hell is eternal because fire has no effect on purging sins. Who is the only one who can purify sin?

> *But now He has reconciled you by Christ's physical body through death to present you holy in His sight, without blemish and free from accusation (Colossians 1:22).*

> *The Son is the radiance of God's glory and the exact representation of His being, sustaining all things by His powerful word. After He had provided purification for sins, He sat down at the right hand of the Majesty in heaven (Hebrews 1:3).*

> *But if we walk in the light, as he is in the light, we have fellowship with one another, and the blood of Jesus, his Son, purifies us from all sin (1 John 1:7).*

Jesus Christ made a promise to the justified thief hanging on a cross next to Him. Did the thief have to go to purgatory to purge his sins or pay a temporal punishment?

> *Jesus answered him, "I tell you the truth, today you will be with me in paradise" (Luke 23:43).*

The Catholic Church teaches that mortal sins can only be forgiven by confessing them to a priest (CCC, para. 1456). Yet, when Christ died, the curtain to the "holy of holies" (that separated God from sinful man) was ripped open from top to bottom. Sinners can now approach God by faith through the shed blood of Jesus. Do sinners need to confess their sins to an exclusive priesthood or can they go directly to Jesus Christ, our High Priest?

> *Therefore He is able to save completely those who come to God through Him, because He always lives to intercede for them (Hebrews 7:25).*

My dear children, I write this to you so that you will not sin. But if anybody does sin, we have one who speaks to the Father in our defense—Jesus Christ, the Righteous One (1 John 2:1).

Only God can forgive sins (Mark 2:7).

Only a mediator or judge can absolve a person from the guilt of sin. The Catholic Church teaches its priests serve as a mediator to absolve sin through the sacrament of Penance (CCC, para. 1424). Since Jesus Christ is the only Mediator, and the only one who can judge the heart, what can be said of those who seek forgiveness in the confessional box? Do they leave with a false hope of forgiveness?

And He has given Him authority to judge because He is the Son of Man (John 5:27).

For there is one God and one mediator between God and men, the man Christ Jesus (1 Timothy 2:5).

What was the mission of Christ?

The Son of Man did not come to be served, but to serve, and to give His life as a ransom for many (Matthew 20:28).

*For the Son of Man came to seek and to save what was lost
(Luke 19:10).*

He was pierced for our transgressions, He was crushed for our iniquities; the punishment that brought us peace was upon Him, and by His wounds we are healed (Isaiah 53:5).

The next day John saw Jesus coming toward him and said, "Look, the Lamb of God, who takes away the sin of the world" (John 1:29).

For God did not send his Son into the world to condemn the world, but to save the world through Him (John 3:17).

I am the good shepherd. The good shepherd lays down His life for the sheep (John 10:11).

For Christ died for sins once for all, the righteous for the unrighteous, to bring you to God. He was put to death in the flesh but made alive by the Spirit (1 Peter 3:18).

The Catholic Church teaches that the mission of Christ continues in the liturgy of the Mass and that "all who die...imperfectly purified....undergo purification, so as to achieve the holiness necessary to enter the joy of heaven" (CCC, para. 1030). Did Jesus say He finished his mission?

"It is finished." With that, He bowed His head and gave up His spirit (John 19:30).

The Roman Catholic Church teaches that those who die in mortal sin go to hell for all eternity (CCC, para. 1035). Since all sins are mortal, who is it that will suffer God's wrath?

Whoever believes in the Son has eternal life, but whoever rejects the Son will not see life, for God's wrath remains on him (John 3:36).

When a sinner has been reconciled to God through the mediation of Jesus Christ, the relationship has changed from one of hostility to one of harmony and peace. What expectations does God have of those who have been reconciled to Him?

God...reconciled us to himself through Christ and gave us the ministry of reconciliation: that God was reconciling the world to Himself in Christ, not counting men's sins against them. And He has committed to us the message of reconciliation. We are therefore Christ's ambassadors, as though God were making His appeal through us. We implore you on Christ's behalf: Be reconciled to God. God made Him who had no sin to be sin for us, so that in Him we might become the righteousness of God (2 Corinthians 5:18–21).

For if, when we were God's enemies, we were reconciled to Him through the death of His Son, how much more, having been reconciled, shall we be saved through His life! Not only is this so, but we also rejoice in God through our Lord Jesus Christ, through whom we have now received reconciliation (Romans 5:10–11).

Redemption is the act of paying the required price necessary to secure the release of one who is being held captive. To redeem someone is to reclaim him or her by paying a ransom. It sets them free! What does Christ redeem us from? At what price?

Christ redeemed us from the curse of the law by becoming a curse for us, for it is written: "Cursed is everyone who is hung on a tree." He redeemed us in order that the blessing given to Abraham might come to the Gentiles through Christ Jesus, so that by faith we might receive the promise of the Spirit. But the Scripture declares that the whole world is a prisoner of sin, so that what was promised, being given through faith in Jesus Christ, might be given to those who believe" (Galatians 3:13–14; 22).

For you know that it was not with perishable things such as silver or gold that you were redeemed from the empty way of life handed down to you from your forefathers, but with the precious blood of Christ, a lamb without blemish or defect (1 Peter 1:18–19).

Our great God and Savior Jesus Christ, who gave himself for us to redeem us from all wickedness and to purify for himself a people that are His very own, eager to do what is good (Titus 2:13–14).

Praise the Lord, O my soul, and forget not all his benefits, who forgives all your sins...who redeems your life from the pit and crowns you with love and compassion (Psalm 103:2–4).

Sinners are saved...

- *from* God's just punishment (2 Thessalonians 1:8–9)
- *by* God's grace, not of works (Ephesians 2:8–9)
- *through* faith in Jesus (John 3:36)
- *because* of God's love & mercy (Titus 3:5, Romans 5:8)
- *only* on the basis of Christ's death and resurrection (1 Corinthians 15:1–4)
- *at* the moment we are born of God (John 1:13)
- *for* God's glory (Ephesians 2:7)
- *throughout* all eternity (Hebrews 5:9, Revelation 22:3–5).

5

The Sacrifice of Jesus

There exists a profound contrast between the teachings of the Bible and the teachings of the Catholic Church concerning the sacrifice of Jesus. The Scriptures reveal: "By one sacrifice He has made perfect forever those who are being made holy. And where these have been forgiven, there is no longer any sacrifice for sin" (Hebrews 10:14, 18). But, according to the Catechism of the Catholic Church:

> *The sacrifice of Jesus and the sacrifice of the Eucharist are one single sacrifice...the same Christ who offered Himself once in a bloody manner on the cross is contained and offered in an unbloody manner on church altars. The Eucharist is thus a sacrifice because it represents (makes present) the sacrifice of the cross and is actually the body and blood, together with the soul and divinity of our Lord Jesus Christ (CCC, para. 1367; 1374).*

Catholics express their faith in the real presence of Christ by worshipping and adoring the wafer as if it were actually God (para. 1378). The Vatican teaches that every time the Mass is celebrated the work of redemption is carried on (para. 1405). Christ, in the Eucharist, is offered repeatedly in reparation for the sins of the living and the dead (para. 1414).

Contrast the Catholic Mass with the worship service of the first century church. What were the four components of their service? Was there a sacrifice offered for sins?

They devoted themselves to the apostles' teaching and to the fellowship, to the breaking of bread and to prayer (Acts 2:42).

The Catechism of the Catholic Church states: "For it is in the liturgy, especially in the divine sacrifice of the Eucharist, that the work of our redemption is accomplished" (para. 1068). "As often as the sacrifice of the Cross by which 'Christ our Pasch has been sacrificed' is celebrated on the altar, the work of our redemption is carried out" (para. 1364).

Do Christians already have redemption or is the work of our redemption still being carried out?

Jesus said, "It is finished" (John 19:30).

For you know that it was not with perishable things such as silver or gold that you were redeemed from the empty way of life handed down to you from your forefathers, but with the precious blood of Christ, a lamb without blemish or defect (1 Peter 1:18).

In Him we have redemption through His blood, the forgiveness of sins, in accordance with the riches of God's grace (Ephesians 1:7).

He did not enter by means of the blood of goats and calves; but He entered the Most Holy Place once for all by His own blood, having obtained eternal redemption (Hebrews 9:12, 26).

The Roman Catholic Church claims the sacrifice of the Mass is a bloodless sacrifice of Jesus. According to the Scriptures, can a blood-less sacrifice have any effect on sin? Can it make atonement for the sin in one's life?

For the life of a creature is in the blood, and I have given it to you to make atonement for yourselves on the altar; it is the blood that makes atonement for one's life (Leviticus 17:11).

In fact, the law requires that nearly everything be cleansed with blood, and without the shedding of blood there is no forgiveness (Hebrews 9:22).

The documents of Vatican Council II state: "In the sacrifice of the Mass Our Lord is immolated." Immolation is the sacrificial killing of a victim. Is it necessary or feasible for Jesus to be killed again?

For we know that since Christ was raised from the dead, He cannot die again; death no longer has mastery over Him. The death He died, He died to sin once for all; but the life He lives, He lives to God (Romans 6:9–10).

Canon I of the Council of Trent states: "If anyone denies that in the sacrament of the most Holy Eucharist are contained truly, really, and substantially the body and blood together with the soul and divinity of our Lord Jesus Christ, and consequently the whole Christ, but says that He is in it only as a sign, let him be anathema." In Paul's directives for the Lord's Supper does he say the substance of the bread has changed? If it had changed into the Body of Christ, would he still call it bread?

For whenever you eat this bread and drink this cup, you proclaim the Lord's death until he comes. Therefore, whoever eats the bread or drinks the cup of the Lord in an unworthy manner will be guilty of sinning against the body and blood of the Lord. A man ought to examine himself before he eats of the bread and drinks of the cup (1 Corinthians 11:26–28).

Transubstantiation is based on the teachings of Aristotle 300 years before Christ. He taught that everything is made up of accidents (outward appearance) and substance (inner essence). Although modern science has proven this theory false, the Catholic Church clings to it and even takes it a step further. They dogmatically claim the inner substance of the wafer changes into the literal body and blood of Jesus while the outer appearance remains the same. The credence for their dogma comes from a literal translation of John 6:25–63.

Do you believe Jesus instructed us to consume Him literally or spiritually? Is He our physical nourishment or spiritual nourishment?

> *The Spirit gives life; the flesh counts for nothing. The words I have spoken to you are spirit and they are life (John 6:63).*

Jesus often spoke to His disciples in figurative language throughout His ministry (John 16:25). What are some of the other figurative descriptions Jesus made of Himself? Did Jesus want us to believe that He was speaking literally in the following verses?

> *Then Jesus declared, "I am the bread of life. He who comes to me will never go hungry, and he who believes in me will never be thirsty" (John 6:35).*

> *When Jesus spoke again to the people, he said, "I am the light of the world. Whoever follows me will never walk in darkness, but will have the light of life" (John 8:12).*

> *I am the gate; whoever enters through me will be saved. He will come in and go out, and find pasture (John 10:9).*

> *"I am the true vine, and my Father is the gardener" (John 15:1).*

Catholics who believe a literal interpretation of John 6 face a serious dilemma. Both the "eating and drinking" and "believing in Jesus" produce the same result–eternal life. What if a person "believes" but does not "eat or drink?" Or what if a person "eats and drinks" but does not "believe?" Does this

person have eternal life because he met one of the requirements but not the other? Would you agree that the only
possible way to harmonize these two verses is to accept one as
literal and the other as figurative?

> *For my Father's will is that everyone who looks to the Son
> and believes in Him shall have eternal life, and I will raise
> him up at the last day" (John 6:40).*

> *Whoever eats my flesh and drinks my blood has eternal
> life, and I will raise him up at the last day (John 6:54).*

Catholics are taught to believe a miracle has occurred when the
inner essence of the host (wafer) is changed into the body and
blood of Christ even though it still looks and tastes like a wafer.
Can you think of any miracle recorded in Scipture that took
place without physical evidence? When Jesus changed water
into wine, did the wine remain under the appearance of water?
Or was it transformed into the best wine at the wedding feast?

> *Then he told them, "Now draw some out and take it to the
> master of the banquet." They did so, and the master of the
> banquet tasted the water that had been turned into wine.
> He did not realize where it had come from, though the
> servants who had drawn the water knew. Then he called
> the bridegroom aside and said, "Everyone brings out the
> choice wine first and then the cheaper wine after the guests
> have had too much to drink; but you have saved the best
> till now" (John 2:8–10).*

God forbids anyone from consuming the blood of a sacrifice. If
Jesus were teaching the multitudes to literally drink His blood,
He would be teaching them to disobey God. How then must
this passage in the 6th chapter of John be interpreted, literally
or figuratively?

> *Any Israelite or any alien living among them who eats
> any blood, I will set my face against that person who eats*

blood and will cut him off from his people. For the life of a creature is in the blood, and I have given it to you to make atonement for yourselves on the altar; it is the blood that makes atonement for one's life. Therefore I say to the Israelites, "None of you may eat blood, nor may an alien living among you eat blood" (Leviticus 17:10–12).

The Catholic Church teaches that Jesus returns physically to the earth each day to be worshipped and sacrificed on its altars. Yet this goes against the teachings of the Bible. According to Scripture, how and where will Jesus return physically to the earth?

"Men of Galilee," they said, "why do you stand here looking into the sky? This same Jesus, who has been taken from you into heaven, will come back in the same way you have seen Him go into heaven" (Acts 1:11).

On that day His feet will stand on the Mount of Olives, east of Jerusalem, and the Mount of Olives will be split in two from east to west, forming a great valley, with half of the mountain moving north and half moving south (Zechariah 14:4).

"So if anyone tells you, 'There He is, out in the desert,' do not go out; or, 'Here He is, in the inner rooms,' do not believe it. For as lightning that comes from the east is visible even in the west, so will be the coming of the Son of Man" (Matthew 24:26–27).

Look, He is coming with the clouds, and every eye will see Him, even those who pierced Him; and all the peoples of the earth will mourn because of Him. So shall it be (Revelation 1:7)!

Propitiation is the turning away of God's wrath against sin because His justice was satisfied at Calvary. Yet Canon 3 of the Council of Trent declares that anyone who does not believe the Sacrifice of the Mass is a propitiatory sacrifice for the sins of the living and the dead is anathema (accursed). Is God's wrath and condemnation appeased when Catholics participate in an ongoing sacrifice or when God declares a sinner righteous on account of his faith in Christ's substitutionary atonement? Is God's wrath and condemnation something a justified Christian still needs to fear?

> *Whoever believes in the Son has eternal life, but whoever rejects the Son will not see life, for God's wrath remains on him" (John 3:36).*

> *Since we have now been justified by His blood, how much more shall we be saved from God's wrath through Him. Therefore, there is now no condemnation for those who are in Christ Jesus (Romans 5:9; 8:1).*

> *For God did not appoint us to suffer wrath but to receive salvation through our Lord Jesus Christ (1 Thessalonians 5:9).*

Consider what the life, death and resurrection of Jesus Christ accomplished.

His life on earth was:

- a revelation of God

- sinless–to be our perfect sacrifice

- righteous–so His righteousness could be given as a gift to those who trust Him

- to testify to truth, to declare His word is truth and to be the personification of truth

- to fulfill over 300 prophecies

His death was:

- to pay–the complete penalty for sin

- to shed His blood–the only remission for sin

- to be a substitute–for sinners
- to satisfy the justice and holy wrath of God–propitiation
- to atone–reconciliation with God
- to redeem–from the bondage and power of sin
- sufficient–nothing else required for salvation
- once for all sin–finished, no more sacrifices

His resurrection:

- declared victory over death, Satan and sin
- proved He is who He said He is
- enables Him to live as our advocate and mediator
- enables Him to impart His life to us
- was the first fruit of the resurrection of saints
- demonstrated the power that is now available for Christians
- to live a victorious life

6

The Righteousness of God

God's holiness and justice demand perfect righteousness for entrance into heaven. Since a sinner has no hope of attaining perfect righteousness, God offers as a gift the perfect righteousness of His Son. This is referred to as the doctrine of justification. Justification is the very heart of the gospel, and a doctrine that separates biblical Christianity from Roman Catholicism. It relates the saving significance of Christ's life and death with God's holy law. God's wisdom is displayed in the way He harmoniously exercises His attributes of holiness, justice, and righteousness along with His attributes of love, mercy, and grace through Jesus.

The *source* of justification is God the Father (Romans 8:33). Since it is impossible for fallen man to meet the righteous standard God's righteousness demands, God offers Christ's righteousness as a gift. Jesus paid a debt He did not owe, because we owe a debt we cannot pay.

The *ground* of justification is the righteousness of Christ. His perfect life and sacrificial death satisfied the demands of God's justice and thus freed God to justify all who believe in Him. Christ's finished work of redemption is the sole ground on which God can pardon sinners (Romans 3:24–26).

The *instrument* of justification is faith (Galatians 3:24). A repentant sinner is imputed with the righteousness of Christ when he believes Jesus is the only way of salvation.

The *principle* of justification is grace (Romans 3:24). We do not merit or deserve to be justified. It is a precious gift from God given freely by His grace. No one is justified by obeying the law (Galatians 3:11).

The *basis* of justification is the blood of Christ (Romans 5:9).

The *recipients* of justification are the wicked, ungodly and unjust persons, not those who deserve it (Romans 4:5).

The *duration* of justification is forever (Romans 8:30).

The *evidence* of justification is good works. Abraham was justified by faith (Genesis 15:6), and the evidence before men was his "works" (James 2:21) when he offered his son. Since one's faith is visible only to God, the evidence to others of justifying faith is good works and obedience to God's Word.

The *fruit* of justification is the words that come from the heart (Matthew 12:35,37).

The *position* of justification is union with Christ. "He made Him who knew no sin to be sin on our behalf that we might become the righteousness of God in Him" (2 Corinthians 5:21). The righteousness of Christ is imputed through His indwelling Spirit.

The *result* of justification is peace with God (Romans 5:1, 2).

The *proof* of a believer's justification is the resurrection of Jesus (Romans 4:25).

The doctrine of justification rests on the basic principles of justice. No judge has the right to declare a guilty person just without justice being served. Can God, as a righteous judge, let the guilty go free without someone paying the punishment?

> *The Lord is slow to anger, abounding in love and forgiving sin and rebellion. Yet He does not leave the guilty unpunished (Numbers 14:18).*
>
> *Acquitting the guilty and condemning the innocent, the Lord detests them both (Proverbs 17:15).*

Who paid the punishment so that God would be just in acquitting sinners of their guilt?

> *But He was pierced for our transgressions, He was crushed for our iniquities; the punishment that brought us peace was upon Him, and by His wounds we are healed (Isaiah 53:5).*

The Catholic Church states that the grace of justification comes through the sacraments, beginning with baptism (CCC, para. 1266), and conforms Catholics to the righteousness of God (CCC, para.1992). Catholics can then merit the graces needed for the attainment of eternal life (CCC, para. 2010) through the sacraments, good works, and obeying the law. Can anyone be justified by good works or obeying the law?

> *All our righteous acts are like filthy rags (Isaiah 64:6).*
>
> *Jesus said to them, "You are the ones who justify yourselves in the eyes of men, but God knows your hearts. What is highly valued among men is detestable in God's sight" (Luke 16:15).*
>
> *However, to the man who does not work but trusts God who justifies the wicked, his faith is credited as righteousness. David says the same thing when he speaks of the blessedness of the man to whom God credits righteousness apart from works (Romans 4:5–6).*
>
> *Clearly no one is justified before God by the law, because, "The righteous will live by faith" (Galatians 3:11).*

You who are trying to be justified by law have been alienated from Christ; you have fallen away from grace (Galatians 5:4).

Catholics are taught that they must establish and maintain their own righteousness to enter heaven rather than seek God's righteousness (CCC, para. 2016, 2027). Is this possible in God's eyes?

As it is written: "There is no one righteous, not even one" (Romans 3:10).

Israel, who pursued a law of righteousness, has not attained it. Why not? Because they pursued it not by faith, but as if it were by works. (Romans 9:31–32).

Brothers, my heart's desire and prayer to God for the Israelites is that they may be saved. For I can testify about them that they are zealous for God, but their zeal is not based on knowledge. Since they did not know the righteousness that comes from God and sought to establish their own, they did not submit to God's righteousness. Christ is the end of the law so that there may be righteousness for everyone who believes (Romans 10:1–4).

(Paul desired) to be found in him, not having a righteousness of my own that comes from the law, but that which is through faith in Christ, the righteousness that comes from God and is by faith (Philippians 3:9).

The Catholic Church teaches that righteousness is infused, from the time of baptism throughout one's life until death, by means of sanctifying grace (CCC, para. 1127-1129, 2023–2024). The Bible reveals that God's righteousness is credited or imputed instantly at the moment of faith. What is a believer's legal position before a holy God?

The words "it was credited to him" were written not for him alone, but also for us, to whom God will credit righ-

teousness, for us who believe in Him who raised Jesus our Lord from the dead (Romans 4:23–24).

The Catholic Church teaches that final justification does not occur until all sins have been purged. Therefore, a Catholic must suffer any unpaid punishment for his sins in purgatory before he can be justified (CCC, para. 1030, 1031). At what moment does the Bible reveal a sinner is justified?

If you confess with your mouth, "Jesus is Lord," and believe in your heart that God raised Him from the dead, you will be saved. For it is with your heart that you believe and are justified, and it is with your mouth that you confess and are saved (Romans 10:9–10).

The Bible teaches that God does not make mistakes; those He justifies, He glorifies. Yet, the Catholic Church teaches that justification can be lost by mortal or grave sin (CCC, para. 1446, 1874). Is justification temporal or permanent? Can anyone ever be condemned after God declares that person righteous?

And those He predestined, He also called; those He called, He also justified; those He justified, He also glorified. What, then, shall we say in response to this? If God is for us, who can be against us? He who did not spare his own Son, but gave Him up for us all—how will He not also, along with Him, graciously give us all things (Romans 8:30–32)?

Blessed is the man whose sin the Lord will never count against him (Romans 4:8).

Canon 30 of the Council of Trent states: "If anyone says that after the reception of the grace of justification the guilt is so remitted and the debt of eternal punishment so blotted out to every repented sinner, that no debt of temporal punishment remains to be discharged in this world or in purgatory before the gates of heaven can be opened, let him be anathema." Does this charge apply to those God has chosen to be justified?

— 51 —

Who will bring any charge against those whom God has chosen? It is God who justifies (Romans 8:33).

Canon 9 of the Council of Trent states: "If anyone says that the sinner is justified by faith alone, meaning that nothing else is required to cooperate in order to obtain the grace of justification...let him be anathema" How does Scripture reveal sinners are justified?

So we, too, have put our faith in Christ Jesus that we may be justified by faith in Christ and not by observing the law, because by observing the law no one will be justified (Galatians 2:16).

The Scripture foresaw that God would justify the Gentiles by faith (Galatians 3:8).

So the law was put in charge to lead us to Christ that we might be justified by faith (Galatians 3:24).

Man's salvation involves justification, sanctification, and glorification. This is why the Bible reveals Christians have been saved, are being saved, and will be saved. Justification removes the "penalty of sin" at the moment we are acquitted by God. Sanctification is the process whereby a Christian overcomes the "power of sin," through the indwelling Holy Spirit, and glorification ultimately removes the Christian from the "presence of sin." For a believer, "justification" is past, "sanctification" is present, and "glorification" is pending or future. Paul was referring to sanctification when he exhorted us "to work out your salvation with fear and trembling" (Philippians 2:12). Notice the verb tenses for "salvation" in the following verses:

He saved us through the washing of rebirth and renewal by the Holy Spirit (Titus 3:5).

For the message of the cross is foolishness to those who are perishing, but to us who are being saved it is the power of God (1 Corinthians 1:18).

Christ was sacrificed once to take away the sins of many people; and He will appear a second time, not to bear sin, but to bring salvation to those who are waiting for Him (Hebrews 9:28).

7

What Must I Do to Be Saved?

When the Philippian jailer asked this question of Paul and Silas, they replied, "Believe in the Lord Jesus, and you will be saved—you and your household" (Acts 16:30–31). What does it mean to believe in the Lord Jesus? Saving faith is composed of knowledge, belief, and trust. A sinner must know and understand certain doctrines from God's Word (Romans 10:17). A sinner must also have the conviction or belief that these doctrines are true (John 16:7–14). And finally a sinner must forsake, or repent of, all efforts to save himself and trust only in the person and work of the Lord Jesus Christ for the complete forgiveness of sins and reconciliation to God (Acts 4:12, Ephesians 2:8–9). Repentance is a change of mind. It is a change of mind from any understanding of God and His plan of redemption that does not conform to the truth of the Scriptures. It comes from a godly sorrow for any and all sins committed. Evidence of genuine faith and repentance is when one turns from a life that is independent of God to a life that is dependent upon Him.

According to Scripture man is born spiritually dead and cannot respond to the gospel without God's initiative. "The man without the Spirit does not accept the things that come from the Spirit of God, for they are foolishness to him and he cannot understand them because they are spiritually discerned" (1 Corinthians 2:14). The Spirit of God, who inspired the writers of

Scripture, must illuminate the hearts of sinners before they can respond to the gospel (Acts 16:14). Only by God's initiative can a sinner be born of the Spirit (John 6:44). In the exercise of His will God brings forth sinners by the word of truth (James 1:18). Man's only hope is to respond to God's calling with repentance and faith.

Many Catholics believe they became children of God because of their baptism with water, or because their parents were of the Catholic faith. Can the faith or will of another person cause someone else to be born of God?

> *Yet to all who received Him, to those who believed in His name, He gave the right to become children of God, children born not of natural descent, nor of human decision or a husband's will, but born of God (John 1:12–13).*

Scripture reveals that no one can come to Jesus without God appointing, calling, and drawing him or her. Yet Catholics believe that they come to Jesus when a priest sprinkles water over them in the sacrament of baptism. Is salvation brought about by an act of God or of man?

> *No one can come to me unless the Father who sent me draws him, and I will raise him up at the last day (John 6:44).*

> *When the Gentiles heard this, they were glad and honored the word of the Lord; and all who were appointed for eternal life believed (Acts 13:48).*

> *For those God foreknew He also predestined to be conformed to the likeness of his Son, that He might be the firstborn among many brothers. And those He predestined, He also called; those He called, He also justified; those He justified, He also glorified (Romans 8:29–30).*

Many of the religious people in the first century rejected Jesus because of their religious pride and self-righteousness. Who is most likely to respond to God's call?

For the Lord takes delight in His people; He crowns the humble with salvation (Psalm 149:4).

God opposes the proud but gives grace to the humble (James 4:6).

But go and learn what this means: "I desire mercy, not sacrifice." For I have not come to call the righteous, but sinners (Matthew 9:13).

Godly sorrow brings repentance that leads to salvation (2 Corinthians 7:10).

If a Roman Catholic (or anyone in any other denomination) is depending upon good works for salvation, he must repent or forsake all efforts to save himself or herself.

He saved us, not because of righteous things we had done, but because of his mercy. He saved us through the washing of rebirth and renewal by the Holy Spirit (Titus 3:5).

For it is by grace you have been saved, through faith—and this not from yourselves, it is the gift of God—not by works, so that no one can boast (Ephesians 2:8–9).

God) has saved us and called us to a holy life—not because of anything we have done, but because of His own purpose and grace (2 Timothy 1:9).

The righteousness and holiness of God demands that sin be punished. Who are the ones who will experience God's wrath?

Whoever rejects the Son will not see life, for God's wrath remains on him (John 3:36).

I told you that you would die in your sins; if you do not believe that I am the one I claim to be, you will indeed die in your sins (John 8:24).

There is a judge for the one who rejects me and does not accept my words; that very word which I spoke will condemn him at the last day (John 12:48).

He will punish those who do not know God and do not obey the Gospel of our Lord Jesus. They will be punished with everlasting destruction and shut out from the presence of the Lord and from the majesty of his power (2 Thessalonians 1:8–9).

What did the Israelites do to avoid the wrath of God? The Passover foreshadows the blood sacrifice of Jesus as the satisfaction of God's wrath. Sinners must trust the blood of Jesus, as the only means of purification, to insure God's wrath will "pass over" them.

> *The blood will be a sign for you on the houses where you are; and when I see the blood, I will pass over you. No destructive plague will touch you when I strike Egypt (Exodus 12:13).*

> *The blood of Jesus, His Son, purifies us from all sin (1 John 1:7).*

> *Since we have now been justified by His blood, how much more shall we be saved from God's wrath through Him (Romans 5:9).*

When does one cross over from eternal damnation to eternal life?

> *Jesus said, "I tell you the truth, whoever hears my word and believes Him who sent me has eternal life and will not be condemned; he has crossed over from death to life" (John 5:24).*

The Apostle Paul wrote about those who might believe in vain. He said only one gospel saves, and that gospel is according to the Scriptures, not tradition. Believing in vain is to trust someone or something other than Jesus Christ, or to believe another gospel according to the traditions of men. Many Catholic traditions, not found in Scripture, nullify the gospel of salvation and cause people to believe in vain.

Now, brothers, I want to remind you of the gospel I preached to you, which you received and on which you have taken your stand. By this gospel you are saved, if you hold firmly to the word I preached to you. Otherwise, you have believed in vain. For what I received I passed on to you as of first importance: that Christ died for our sins according to the Scriptures, that he was buried, that he was raised on the third day according to the Scriptures (1 Corinthians 15:1–4).

Many who "profess" Jesus Christ do not "possess" Jesus Christ because they have not been truly converted. There are several examples of spurious faith in the New Testament. Jesus spoke of temporary faith (Matthew 13:1–23); James talked of dead faith and the devil's faith; Paul talked of believing in vain (1 Corinthians 15:2); Simon the Sorcerer believed for the wrong reasons (Acts 8:9–24); and those who called Jesus "Lord" were told to depart from Him (Matthew 7:21–23). How would you define "saving" faith? Is it mere head knowledge, or does it include believing with heartfelt conviction?

If you confess with your mouth, "Jesus is Lord," and believe in your heart that God raised him from the dead, you will be saved. For it is with your heart that you believe and are justified, and it is with your mouth that you confess and are saved (Romans 10:9–10).

Here are some indicators of counterfeit or spurious faith. Those who desire to be saved from the punishment of sin, but not from sin itself. Those who desire the blessings of Christ, but not a relationship with Him. Those who desire the free gift of eternal life, but not with empty hands of faith. Those who desire Jesus Christ as a priest to procure pardon and peace, but not as a prophet to instruct them or as a king to rule over them. And, finally, those who desire Jesus Christ, but only under the terms of their religious traditions or unbending philosophy.

What Scriptural advice would you give someone who appears to have a counterfeit faith?

Examine yourselves to see whether you are in the faith; test yourselves. Do you not realize that Christ Jesus is in you, unless, of course, you fail the test? (2 Corinthians 13:5). Therefore, my brothers, be all the more eager to make your calling and election sure (2 Peter 1:10).

There are many voices that say they are speaking for God, but the voice of the Shepherd is heard through His Word. How can you be sure you have been born again of the Holy Spirit?

The Spirit himself testifies with our spirit that we are God's children (Romans 8:16).

Jesus said, "His sheep follow him because they know his voice. But they will never follow a stranger; in fact, they will run away from him because they do not recognize a stranger's voice. . . .I am the good shepherd; I know my sheep and my sheep know me (John 10:4, 5, 14).

Have you ever received God's gift of eternal life? Do you know if all your sins are completely forgiven? Do you know if you have been reconciled to God? If not, why not forsake all attempts to save yourself, repent from your dead works and put all your trust and confidence in the Lord Jesus Christ?

Summary

Clearly it is impossible to adhere to the dogmas of the Catholic Church and, at the same time, believe the gospel. The two faiths are mutually exclusive. If a Catholic adheres to the dogmas of his church, he is condemned by the Word of God (John 12:48), whereas if a Catholic believes the Word of God, he is condemned with an anathema by his church. Catholics must place all their trust in the life, death, and resurrection of Jesus for their salvation. This means repenting from the things that cannot save them and trusting the only One who can. The work of redemption is finished and the sacrifice of Christ is sufficient. We are all exhorted to destroy all arguments and traditions that oppose the revealed knowledge of God and take every thought captive to the obedience of Christ (2 Corinthians 10:5).

8

The Assurance of Eternal Life

The gospel is the good news of eternal life and is based on God's justice and faithfulness in keeping His promises (1 John 1:9). Eternal life means life is eternal, and those who possess it cannot die. Eternal life is eternal because the very life of Jesus Christ is imparted to Christians, and Jesus can never die again (Romans 6:9–10). Jesus is able to save those who come to God through Him completely and forever because He has defeated death (1 Corinthians 15:54–57). When a repentant sinner has faith in God's promises and believes Jesus has done all that is necessary for salvation, he has assurance. God promises that believers will not come into judgment because Jesus bore their sins and judgment on the cross. Yet the Catholic Church teaches: "If anyone says that he will for certain, with an absolute and infallible certainty, have that great gift of perseverance even to the end...let him be anathema" (Canon 16, Trent). If man were only saved until his next serious sin, Christ's work of redemption would only be temporal, but God says that it is eternal (Hebrews 5:9). Whenever man is involved in attaining and/or preserving his salvation, there can never be assurance. However, when one believes the objective truth of the gospel, he will be more certain of living eternally in heaven than of living one more day on earth.

The very nature of eternal life means it is eternal. The gift of eternal life can never be terminated, lost, or revoked. No one can die again spiritually after receiving eternal life.

> *I tell you the truth, whoever hears my word and believes Him who sent me has eternal life and will not be condemned; he has crossed over from death to life (John 5:24). God's gifts and his calling are irrevocable (Romans 11:29). God has given us eternal life, and this life is in His Son. He who has the Son has life; he who does not have the Son of God does not have life (1 John 5:11–12).*

> *Therefore, there is now no condemnation for those who are in Christ Jesus (Romans 8:1).*

After Jesus paid the penalty and punishment of sin with His death, He was resurrected to impart His life to believers. Jesus now lives to intercede for those who trust Him as the all-sufficient Savior.

> *My dear children, I write this to you so that you will not sin. But if anybody does sin, we have one who speaks to the Father in our defense—Jesus Christ, the Righteous One (1 John 2:1).*

> *Therefore He is able to save completely those who come to God through Him, because He always lives to intercede for them (Hebrews 7:25).*

God does not count the sins of Christians against them or take away their salvation. All the sins of believers (past and future) have been imputed to Christ. However, when a believer sins, he can expect discipline from a loving Father.

> *Blessed is the man whose sin the Lord will never count against him (Romans 4:8).*

> *The Lord disciplines those He loved...For what son is not disciplined by his father? If you are not disciplined (and everyone undergoes discipline), then you are illegitimate children and not true sons (Hebrews 12:6–8).*

The gift of eternal life is secured on the faithfulness and promises of God, and not the faithfulness of the believer. Only if man is involved in attaining or preserving his salvation can there be no assurance. Since man does nothing to earn salvation, he can do nothing to lose it.

> *I give them eternal life, and they shall never perish; no one can snatch them out of my hand. My Father, who has given them to me, is greater than all; no one can snatch them out of my Father's hand. I and the Father are one (John 10:28–30).*

> *And those He predestined, He also called; those He called, He also justified; those He justified, He also glorified (Romans 8:30).*

> *To Him who is able to keep you from falling and to present you before His glorious presence without fault and with great joy (Jude 24).*

> *Praise be to the God and Father of our Lord Jesus Christ! In his great mercy He has given us new birth into a living hope through the resurrection of Jesus Christ from the dead, and into an inheritance that can never perish, spoil or fade, kept in heaven for you, who through faith are shielded by God's power until the coming of the salvation that is ready to be revealed in the last time (1 Peter 1:3–5).*

> *And this is the will of Him who sent me, that I shall lose none of all that He has given me, but raise them up at the last day (John 6:39).*

Roman Catholicism teaches that the sin of presumption is committed when anyone claims to know he has eternal life. "If anyone says that after the reception of the grace of justification, the guilt is so remitted and the debt of eternal punishment so blotted out, to every repentant sinner, that no debt of temporal punishment remains to be discharged in this world or in purgatory before the gates of heaven can be opened, let him be anathema" (Canon 30, 6th session, Trent). How does this teaching compare with the Word of God?

I write these things to you who believe in the name of the Son of God so that you may know that you have eternal life (1 John 5:13).

Part 2

A Study of Contrasts

9

Religion vs. Relationship

The Apostle Paul exchanged his religion for an everlasting relationship with the Lord Jesus Christ. He considered all of his religious accomplishments worthless rubbish for the sake of knowing Christ Jesus. If anyone had reason to boast and be proud of his religious status it was Paul, "a Hebrew of Hebrews; as to the Law, a Pharisee; as to zeal, a persecutor of the church; as to the righteousness which is in the Law, found blameless" (Philippians 3:5–6). Yet he considered all this contemptible compared to changing his relationship with God from one of enmity and hostility to one of peace and harmony (Philippians 3:7–11; Colossians 1:20). The notable religious credentials that he once thought profitable were actually worthless and damning to his soul (Luke 18:9–14).

The Bondage of Religion

True disciples of Jesus are those who have been set free by the truth as they abide in His Word (John 8:31–32). Those who do not know the truth will continue to be enslaved to the bondage of religion. Throughout history, the goal of every false religion has been to control people. This has been accomplished with religious traditions, legalism, pride, and deception. One example of this fierce religious loyalty is a comment we hear so often from Roman Catholics: "I was born a Catholic and I will die a Catholic." They need to know that true conversion only takes place when they confess: "I was born a sinner and will die a saint." And what a way to die! By God's amazing grace, saints are elected in Christ (Ephesians 1:4), called to Christ (1 Corinthians 1:9), have believed the truth about Christ (Romans 10:14–17), have turned to Christ in repentance (1 Peter 2:25), are justified by the blood of Christ (Romans 5:9), are united with Christ (Galatians 2:20), are being transformed into the image of Christ (2 Corinthians 3:18), are being kept and preserved by Christ (1 John 5:18), and will one day gain the glory of Christ (2 Thessalonians 2:14). Why would anyone choose to be enslaved to religion when they can become a blessed and privileged slave of the Lord Jesus?

The End of Religion

The Lord Jesus Christ never came to start a religion; in fact, He put an end to the only religion God ever ordained. Since Christianity in its purest form is not a religion, but a relationship with God through Jesus Christ, Judaism is the only religion ordained by God. All the other religions of the world have their origin in the minds of men who were influenced by God's adversaries. When Jesus Christ, the Jewish Messiah, gave up His Spirit on Calvary's cross, no longer were religious priests needed to offer sacrifices to God. Anyone could now have access to the Father through the Son by faith in His once for all sacrifice for sin. Ironically, the rulers of this God-ordained religion had become so corrupt that they plotted to murder their Messiah (John 11:53). After the Lord's death and resurrection there was no more need for religion. Jesus, the perfect and eternal High Priest, offered Himself, the perfect sacrifice, to a perfect God who demands perfection. The veil that once separated sinners from their holy God was torn open from top to bottom (Matthew 27:51). The one Mediator between God and man now provides access to the Father (1 Timothy 2:5). By faith in the shed blood of Jesus, repentant sinners can enter into the presence of God with confidence (Hebrews 10:19–20). No more religion, no more priests offering sacrifices for sin, and no more religious rituals or ceremonies are required. In place of religion, the risen Savior mediates a relationship with God through faith in His one sacrifice for all sin, for all time (Hebrews 10:10–18).

Christianity, in its purest form, is not a religion, but a Spirit-sealed relationship with the God of all creation. Roman Catholicism is a corrupted form of Christianity. It became corrupt when it denied the finished and all-sufficient work of Jesus and perverted His gospel. This gospel of works leads people to a Christ-less eternity. True Christianity instructs people to study the Bible and believe what God says. Religion, on the other hand, requires people to believe what man says God says. When people without discernment submit to men who are naturally prone to error, they are easily deceived. Catholicism tries to overcome this by declaring its popes to be infallible in matters of faith. True Christianity is when God's children follow the Lord Jesus, who is the only one immune from error. I will never forget what my uncle, a Catholic priest of 58 years, said after I read to him Scriptures refuting Catholic traditions. He said, "God doesn't really mean what He says there; let me tell you what He means."

The Deception of Religion

When you ask most religious people what they are trusting to gain entrance into heaven, they rarely mention the name of Jesus. That's because their religion is the supreme object of their faith. They trust their self-righteous clergy and their religious works and rituals to keep them heaven bound. Tragically, they cannot see the glory and sufficiency of Christ Jesus. They have been blinded from the truth of the gospel by religious indoctrination, a most effective tool of Satan (2 Corinthians 4:4). His primary goal is to confuse people by corrupting and distorting truth as much as possible. Many victims of religious indoctrination are content to blindly trust their unregenerate spiritual rulers, who are willfully and woefully ignorant of biblical doctrine, and are more interested in holding onto their power than seeking the truth. We have found that indoctrination is so powerful that many Catholics refuse to engage in conversations about spiritual issues with non-Catholics. I recall, as a young indoctrinated Catholic, how "lucky" and proud I was to be born into what I was told to be the one true church. I felt sorry for Protestants who were not as "lucky" as I was. So, blinded by Catholic traditions, I did not realize my zeal was misdirected. I was honoring God with my lips, but I was submitting to another Lord—the pope.

The Attraction of Religion

One of the primary attractions of a religion is its appeal to the flesh. The world tells us that "seeing is believing," that we must see before we can believe. This explains why it is so easy for religious people to believe what they can see or touch. Catholics worship and consume the Eucharist, a "god" they can see. They go to a priest they can see to receive sacraments they can see to merit the graces necessary for salvation. They light votive candles as a visible sign of their offerings. And, yes, they bow down and pray toward statues they can see.

Those who have a relationship with their Savior walk by faith, not by sight (2 Corinthians 5:7). Since faith is the conviction of things not seen, we fix our eyes not on what is seen, but on what is unseen. For what is seen is temporary, but what is unseen is eternal (Hebrews 11:1; 2 Corinthians 4:18). Jesus said only those who believe will see the glory of God (John 11:40).

All religions teach that you must do things to appease their god or gods. Every false religion has a works-based system of righteousness that instructs its followers as to what they must do to achieve spiritual blessings. This checklist mentality appeals to the natural man, but man's best efforts are but filthy rags in the sight of a holy God (Isaiah 64:6). Many do their good works because of their zeal for God, but they are ignorant of what God's righteousness demands (Romans 10:1–4). Christianity is set apart from all religions because its Founder has done everything necessary for repenting sinners to have a right relationship with God. Spiritual blessings are available by God's grace to all who trust what Jesus Christ has accomplished through His sinless life, death, and resurrection. All religions say, "DO." True Christianity says, "DONE." Those who desire an eternal relationship with God must trust in what has been *done* by the Lord Jesus, apart from anything they *do* for Him (Ephesians 2:8–9).

The Loyalty of Religion

Religion stirs up a passionate loyalty to its rulers instead of to the Lord Jesus Christ. Who can forget the images of Pope John Paul II's funeral? Thousands of misguided Catholics stood in long lines for up to 18 hours to venerate a dead man with an unbiblical rosary in his hands and a twisted crucifix by his side. What a sharp contrast to those who have an everlasting relationship with the *only* Holy Father. They refuse to listen to the voice of robbers who are out to steal and destroy their souls. They flee from them and instead follow the voice of the Good Shepherd who gave His life for His sheep and calls them by name (John 10:3–11). They come to Him for eternal life, mourning over the sins that nailed Him to the cross. They recognize their unworthiness to be in His presence, yet they rejoice in the hope they have in His Word (Psalm 130:5). Christ and His Word are so connected that one cannot have a relationship with Him apart from His Word (John 8:47).

Those who desire to have a relationship with the true God must seek Him from the only infallible source for truth. All religious teachings, including the teachings in this book, must be tested for veracity by searching the Scriptures (Acts 17:11). Those who cling to religious teachings while rejecting God's Word will be condemned on the last day by the very Word they rejected (John 12:48). Conversely, those who believe the Scriptures have been born again through the incorruptible seed that is the Word of God (1 Peter 1:23). As children of God, it is their ambition to be pleasing to the one who set them free from the bondage of religion (2 Corinthians 5:9–10).

Everyone must take the same approach Jesus did by refuting religious error and opposing those who spread it. Religion can never save anyone; in fact, it cuts them off from God and the saving power of the gospel (Romans 1:16; 4:2–8). May God help those who are enslaved to their worthless and empty religions to become privileged slaves of the Lord Jesus Christ.

10

God's Truth vs. Satan's Lies

The Roman Catholic Church claims to be the one true church founded by Jesus Christ. But is it really? Or has it become Satan's most cleverly disguised counterfeit? To the casual observer the Roman Catholic Church appears to be genuinely Christian because it upholds the basic fundamentals of Christianity. Keep in mind, however, that the most deceptive counterfeit is the one that most closely resembles the genuine article. Catholicism's veil of truth covers a false gospel—a gospel of works. It is "good works" that Satan uses in all of man's religions to thwart the saving power of God's grace. The great lie of Satan is that man can appease God's justice and wrath by performing good works. It is a most deadly lie, because man's works nullify God's grace—the only means by which God saves sinners (Ephesians 2:8–9).

Thus, the battle for the eternal destiny of souls is ultimately a conflict between God's truth and Satan's lies. Satan seduces humanity with cleverly created counterfeits that blind people from the truth. "The god of this age (Satan) has blinded the minds of unbelievers, so that they cannot see the light of the gospel of the glory of Christ, who is the image of God" (2 Corinthians 4:4). As the prince of the world, he holds men captive with his lies. Only the truth of God can set men free (John 8:31).

In order to overcome Satan's deception we must study and understand his character, his mission, and his weapons as they are revealed in Scripture. Jesus described Satan's character as "a murderer from the beginning, not holding to the truth, for there is no truth in him. When he lies, he speaks his native language, for he is a liar and the father of lies. Yet because I tell the truth, you do not believe me" (John 8:44-45). Satan's mission from the beginning has been to deceive. "Eve was deceived by the serpent's cunning" (2 Corinthians 11:3). Peter warns us of the danger he represents. "Your enemy the devil prowls around like a roaring lion looking for someone to devour" (1 Peter 5:8).

Satan uses many counterfeits to deceive the world. He himself is a counterfeit god.

> *He will oppose and will exalt himself over everything that is called God or is worshiped, so that he sets himself up in God's temple, proclaiming himself to be God (2 Thessalonians 2:4).*

Satan also deceives the world with a counterfeit Jesus and a counterfeit gospel. The deception is so clever that the church puts up with it.

> *For if someone comes to you and preaches a Jesus other than the Jesus we preached, or if you receive a different spirit from the one you received, or a different gospel from the one you accepted, you put up with it easily enough (2 Corinthians 11:4).*

Another counterfeit Satan uses is idolatry in the place of true worship. This occurs when people exchange the truth of God for a lie (Romans 1:23). Roman Catholics worship the Eucharist because they have been taught that it has become God through the miracle of transubstantiation. They believe Jesus Christ has become physically present in the wafer. Counterfeit worship occurs when people do not know the true God and His Word.

You Samaritans worship what you do not know; we worship what we do know, for salvation is from the Jews. God is spirit, and his worshipers must worship in spirit and in truth (John 4:22, 24).

Given that the Eucharist is a counterfeit Christ and transubstantiation is a counterfeit sign, we are not surprised when the Roman Catholic Church calls its bishops the successors of the apostles. The Bible warns us that Satan uses false Christs, false prophets, and false apostles, empowered by counterfeit signs and wonders, to deceive many.

For many will come in my name, claiming, 'I am the Christ,' and will deceive many...and many false prophets will appear and deceive many people (Matthew 24:5, 11).

For false Christs and false prophets will appear and perform great signs and miracles to deceive even the elect, if that were possible (Matthew 24:24).

The coming of the lawless one will be in accordance with the work of Satan displayed in all kinds of counterfeit miracles, signs and wonders (2 Thessalonians 2:9).

For such men are false apostles, deceitful workman, masquerading as apostles of Christ (2 Corinthians 11:13).

But there were also false prophets among the people, just as there will be false teachers among you. They will secretly introduce destructive heresies, even denying the sovereign Lord who bought them—bringing swift destruction on themselves. Many will follow their shameful ways and will bring the way of truth into disrepute (2 Peter 2:1–2).

False teachers will deceive and confuse many because they appear as servants of righteousness. Paul warned us that these deceivers would even come from within the church.

I know that after I leave, savage wolves will come in among you and will not spare the flock. Even from your

own number men will arise and distort the truth in order to draw away disciples after them (Acts 20:29–30).
There will be false teachers among you (2 Peter 2:1).
Evidently some people are throwing you into confusion and are trying to pervert the gospel of Christ (Galatians 1:7).
It is not surprising, then, if his (Satan) servants masquerade as servants of righteousness (2 Corinthians 11:15).

Many people are deceived because they seek teachers who appeal to the flesh and who tickle their ears. One of the great Catholic myths is the teaching of purgatory. Catholics are taught that many of their sins are not serious enough to warrant the eternal fires of hell, but only the temporal fires of purgatory.

For the time will come when men will not put up with sound doctrine. Instead, to suit their own desires, they will gather around them a great number of teachers to say what their itching ears want to hear. They will turn their ears away from the truth and turn aside to myths (2 Timothy 4:3–4).

The Spirit clearly says that in later times some will abandon the faith and follow deceiving spirits and things taught by demons (1 Timothy 4:1).

Deceptive religious leaders control people by holding them captive with legalistic tradition. For such people are not serving our Lord Christ, but their own appetites. By smooth talk and flattery they deceive the minds of naive people (Romans 16:18). Paul warned us about these deceivers. See to it that no one takes you captive through hollow and deceptive philosophy, which depends on human tradition and the basic principles of this world rather than on Christ (Colossians 2:8).

One of the most deceptive schemes of Satan has been the use of apparitions, or supernatural visions. In 1531 apparitions of Mary began appearing in various parts of the world. The best known are Guadalupe, Mexico 1531, La Salette, France 1846,

Lourdes, France 1858, Fatima, Portugal 1917, and Medjugorje, Bosnia-Herzegovina 1981. One apparition of Mary gave this message: "To save people from going to hell, God wishes to establish in the world the devotion to my immaculate heart. If people do what I tell you many souls will be saved and there will be peace." Another apparition said: "Many souls go to hell because they have no one to pray and make sacrifices for them." Knowing that Satan can appear as an angel of light, we must test every spirit. It is inconceivable that Mary would ever preach a different gospel that would deny the sacrifice of her Son.

> *But even if we or an angel from heaven should preach a gospel other than the one we preached to you, let him be eternally condemned (Galatians 1:8).*

We can learn from Jesus in the way He responded to Satan. He used the Scriptures as the authority, and a powerful weapon to rebuke the devil. After each of Satan's attempts to deceive, the Lord responds with "it is written" (Matthew 4:4, 7, 10).

With all these biblical warnings about Satan and deception, how can we discern which teachings are true? We must heed the exhortation of Jesus and follow the example of the Bereans.

> *Jesus said, "If you hold to my teaching, you are really my disciples. Then you will know the truth, and the truth will set you free" (John 8:31–32).*

> *Now the Bereans were of more noble character than the Thessalonians, for they received the message with great eagerness and examined the Scriptures every day to see if what Paul said was true (Acts 17:11).*

Once we know certain teachings are false or deceptive, what are we to do?

> *We demolish arguments and every pretension that sets itself up against the knowledge of God, and we take captive every thought to make it obedient to Christ (2 Corinthians 10:5).*

Have nothing to do with godless myths and old wives'
tales (1 Timothy 4:7).

How can we avoid being deceived and seduced by the schemes of the devil? We must follow the exhortations of Paul. *Do your best to present yourself to God as one approved...who correctly handles the word of truth* (2 Timothy 2:15). And most importantly:

> *Put on the full armor of God so that you can take your stand against the devil's schemes. For our struggle is not against flesh and blood, but against the rulers, against the authorities, against the powers of this dark world and against the spiritual forces of evil in the heavenly realms. Stand firm then, with the belt of truth buckled around your waist, with the breastplate of righteousness in place, and with your feet fitted with the readiness that comes from the gospel of peace. In addition to all this, take up the shield of faith, with which you can extinguish all the flaming arrows of the evil one. Take the helmet of salvation and the sword of the Spirit, which is the Word of God. And pray in the Spirit on all occasions with all kinds of prayers and requests (Ephesians 6:11–12, 14–18).*

11

The Mary of Catholicism vs. The Mary of the Bible

The role of Mary in the Catholic Church is dramatically different from her role in biblical history. According to the Catholic Encyclopedia, the first prophecy referring to Mary is found in Genesis 3:15 where the Catholic Douay-Reims Bible states the woman herself will win the victory over Satan. It reads: "I will put enmities between thee and the woman, and thy seed and her seed; *she* shall crush thy head, and thou shalt lie in wait for *her* heel." The Hebrew text reads "he" (referring to Jesus) as the one who would crush the serpent's head. The Catholic Catechism teaches: "Mary did not lay aside this saving office, but by her manifold intercession continues to bring us the gifts of eternal salvation" (CCC, para. 969). "The Immaculate Virgin, preserved free from all stain of original sin, when the course of her earthly life was finished, was taken up body and soul into heavenly glory, and exalted by the Lord as Queen over all things. In giving birth you kept your virginity. You conceived the living God and, by your prayers, will deliver our souls from death" (CCC, para. 966). She is to be praised with special devotion (CCC, para, 971). Mary, "by special grace of God, committed no sin of any kind during her whole earthly life" (CCC, para.411). The Catholic Church promises that all those who seek Mary's protection will be saved for all eternity. These doctrines have robbed God of His glory and have resulted in Catholics often showing greater devotion to Mary than to Christ.

Catholicism teaches that Mary is the mother of God, but Mary is no more the mother of God than Joseph is the father of Jesus.

In the *Fundamentals of Catholic Dogma*, Dr. Ludwig Ott states: "In the power of the grace of Redemption merited by Christ, Mary, by her spiritual entering into the sacrifice of her Divine Son for men, made atonement for the sins of men, and…merited the application of the redemptive grace of Christ. In this manner she co-operates in the subjective redemption of mankind" (page 213). Here the Catholic Church is claiming that Mary made atonement for the sins of men!

The Catholic exaltation of Mary diminishes the sufficiency of Christ and the integrity of the gospel. "Devotion to the Blessed Virgin is intrinsic to Christian worship" (CCC, 971). God alone is exalted above heaven and earth, and He alone is to receive all honor and praise.

> *Let them praise the name of the Lord, for His name alone is exalted; His splendor is above the earth and the heavens (Psalm 148:13).*

> *Then I heard every creature in heaven and on earth and under the earth and on the sea, and all that is in them, singing: "To Him who sits on the throne and to the Lamb be praise and honor and glory and power, for ever and ever" (Revelation 5:13)!*

Throughout biblical history, prayer is directed only to God. Yet Catholics are encouraged to pray to Mary and the saints. Many more Catholic Churches are named after Mary than after Jesus. Statues of Mary are very visible and prominent in Catholic Churches. Many Catholics bow down to them as they pray. Is this an offense to God?

> *You shall not make for yourself an idol in the form of anything in heaven above or on the earth beneath or in the waters below. You shall not bow down to them or*

worship them; for I, the Lord your God, am a jealous God (Exodus 20:4–5).

Let no one be found among you...who consults the dead. Anyone who does these things is detestable to the Lord (Deuteronomy 18:10–12).

The Catholic Church teaches that Mary was a virgin before, during, and after the birth of Christ (CCC, para. 496-511). Yet there are many biblical passages to the contrary, such as Matthew 12:47, 13:55–56, John 7:5, Acts 1:14, 1 Corinthians 9:5, and Galatians 1:19. Catholics argue the references to brothers of Jesus should be interpreted as relatives. However, the word "brother" is the Greek word *adelphos*, which is the common word to describe blood brothers. In Matthew 13:56 the feminine *adelphe* is used to describe Jesus' sisters. If these were cousins, the Holy Spirit could have used the Greek word *anepsios* as He does in Colossians 4:10 (the only place where it is found in the New Testament) to describe Barnabas' cousin Mark, or the word *suggenes*, which is often used to describe relatives in general (Acts 7:14). Mary's perpetual virginity goes against Scripture.

In a Messianic psalm, in a reference to Jesus the Psalmist wrote: "I am a stranger to my brothers, an alien to my own mother's sons" (Psalm 69:8).

Speaking of Joseph on the subject of sexual relations, Matthew wrote:

> *"But he had no union with her until she gave birth to a son. And he gave him the name Jesus" (Matthew 1:25).*

> *Isn't this the carpenter's son? Isn't his mother's name Mary, and aren't his brothers James, Joseph, Simon and Judas? Aren't all his sisters with us? Where then did this man get all these things? (Matthew 13:55–56).*

Catholics are also taught that Mary was preserved from original sin and lived a perfectly sinless life. "She did so in order to serve the mystery of redemption with Him…being obedient she became the cause of salvation for herself and for the whole human race" (CCC, para. 494). She is referred to as "the All-Holy One" (CCC, para. 2677).

Mary acknowledged her need for a Savior by her prayer, "my spirit rejoices in God my Savior" (Luke 1:47). Paul declared, "for all have sinned and fall short of the glory of God" (Romans 3:23).

According to the Catholic Catechism, Mary "did not lay aside [her] saving office, but by her manifold intercession continues to bring us the gifts of eternal salvation." She "is Advocate and Mediatrix" (CCC, para. 969). Her "prayers will deliver our souls from death." (CCC, para. 966) What is the spiritual danger for Catholics when they look to Mary instead of Jesus?

> *But I am afraid that just as Eve was deceived by the serpent's cunning, your minds may somehow be led astray from your sincere and pure devotion to Christ (2 Corinthians 11:3).*

> *Let us fix our eyes on Jesus, the author and perfecter of our faith, who for the joy set before him endured the cross, scorning its shame, and sat down at the right hand of the throne of God (Hebrews 12:2).*

The motto of Pope John Paul II was *Totus Tuus*, which means "totally yours," and refers to his total consecration to Mary. The motto is personally lived and highly recommended by the pope. He said, "I belong to you entirely, and all that I possess is yours, Virgin blessed above all." How does the pope's consecration line up with the words of Christ?

> *As Jesus was saying these things, a woman in the crowd called out, "Blessed is the mother who gave you birth and nursed you." He replied, "Blessed rather are those who hear the word of God and obey it" (Luke 11:27–28).*

Did Jesus give His mother any special position in relation to other believers?

While Jesus was still talking to the crowd, his mother and brothers stood outside, wanting to speak to him. Someone told him, "Your mother and brothers are standing outside, wanting to speak to you." He replied to him, "Who is my mother, and who are my brothers?" Pointing to his disciples, he said, "Here are my mother and my brothers. For whoever does the will of my Father in heaven is my brother and sister and mother" (Matthew 12:46–50).

Centuries before Christ, the pagan world worshipped a mother god with a baby god in her arms. The Egyptian Madonna, Isis, carrying her little Sun god, Horus, became so popular that this mother-goddess supplanted the worship of the father god. Once Mary was proclaimed "Queen of Heaven" the very statues of Isis were carried from vacant pagan temples and installed as Christian Madonnas in the churches of Rome. Mary is never mentioned in the Bible after the first chapter of Acts, and there is no scriptural support for many of the Catholic doctrines on Mary.

Medieval piety in the West developed the prayer of the rosary (CCC, para. 2678). The rosary consists of 53 repetitious prayers to Mary, six prayers to God, the Father, and six prayers to the Trinity. Did Jesus encourage or forbid this type of practice?

And when you pray, do not keep on babbling like pagans, for they think they will be heard because of their many words (Matthew 6:7).

Apparitions (supernatural visions) of Mary are synonymous with an orthodox adherence to the doctrines, rites, and traditional practices of the Roman Catholic Church. Many Catholic theologians believe that Our Lady's Messages are uniquely designed for the difficult and trying times in which we live today, and suggest they are interventions to save the world from war, hunger, and eternal damnation. These messages that the Roman Catholic Church attributes to Mary go directly against the Bible.

> "You saw hell where the souls of poor sinners go. In order to save them, God wishes to establish devotion to my Immaculate Heart in the world. If people do what I ask, many souls will be saved and there will be peace. Only I can help you. My Immaculate Heart will be your refuge and the way that will lead you to God. In the end, My Immaculate Heart will triumph." (Fatima)

> "Take this Scapular. Whosoever dies wearing it shall not suffer eternal fire. It shall be a sign of salvation, a protection in danger, and a pledge of peace." (Mt. Carmel)

> "If my people do not wish to submit themselves, I am forced to let go of the hand of my Son. It is so heavy and weighs me down so much I can no longer keep hold of it. I have suffered all the time for the rest of you! If you do not wish my Son to abandon you, I must take it upon myself to pray for you continually. I gave you six days to work, I kept the seventh for myself, and no one wishes to grant it to me. This is what weighs down the arm of my Son so much." (La Salette)

What warnings have we been given from God's Word that may apply to these apparitions?

> *And no wonder, for Satan himself masquerades as an angel of light (2 Corinthians 11:14).*

> *Because of the signs he was given power to do on behalf of the first beast, he deceived the inhabitants of the earth (Revelation 13:14).*

Compare the attributes of Jesus Christ with the attributes the Roman Catholic Church gives to Mary. They are often the same.

<u>The Lord Jesus Christ</u>	<u>The Catholic Version of Mary</u>
Conceived of the Holy Spirit	Immaculately conceived
The Son of God	The Mother of God
Born without sin	Born without sin
Committed no sin	Committed no sin
Suffered on Calvary's cross	Suffered at Calvary's cross
Bodily ascended into glory	Bodily assumed into glory
King of Heaven	Queen of Heaven
Prince of Peace	Queen of peace
Source of grace	Channel of all grace
Redeemer	Co-redeemer
Mediator	Mediatrix
Advocate	Advocate
Second Adam	Second Eve

12

Catholicism's Traditions vs. God's Word

Every one who names the name of Christ is faced with a most important choice—in whom will I trust for my eternal destiny? Will it be the teachings and traditions of men or will it be the Word of God? The decision is a critical one because of the many Scriptural warnings concerning deception. The Apostle Paul wrote: "Savage wolves will come in among you and will not spare the flock. Even from your own number men will arise and distort the truth in order to draw away disciples after them. So be on your guard! Remember that for three years I never stopped warning each of you night and day with tears" (Acts 20:29–31). Regarding the traditions of men he wrote: "See to it that no one takes you captive through hollow and deceptive philosophy, which depends *on human tradition* and the basic principles of this world *rather than on Christ*" (Colossians 2:8). Jesus strongly rebuked the Jewish religious leaders of His day for nullifying the Word of God with their traditions. He said, "They worship Me in vain; their teachings are but rules taught by men. You have let go of the commands of God and are holding on to the *traditions of men*." And He said to them, "You have a fine way of setting aside the commands of God in order to observe your own traditions…Thus you *nullify the Word* of God by your tradition that you have handed down" (Mark 7:7–13).

For hundreds of years the religious leaders of the Catholic Church have been nullifying the Word of God with their own traditions. These traditions do one of three things. They either: (1) directly oppose the Word of God; (2) distort the Word of God; or (3) are not supported by the Word of God. Nevertheless, in the Catholic Church "both Scripture and Tradition must be accepted and honored with equal sentiments of devotion and reverence" (CCC, para. 82). Following are some Catholic Traditions that nullify the Word of God (numbers in parenthesis refer to paragraph numbers from the *Catechism of the Catholic Church*).

Anathema, A Solemn Condemnation
(*Council of Trent, Vatican Council II*)

This Catholic tradition was established in the 16th century as a means to counter the Protestant Reformation. The Catholic Church turned certain people over to God for condemnation. Today they pronounce over 100 condemnations on those who do not believe the dogmas of the Catholic Church.

"Anathema" is used only twice in the New Testament. An anathema is pronounced on those who preach a different gospel and on those who do not love God (Galatians 1:6–9; 1 Corinthians 16:22).

Apostolic Succession to Expound Divine Revelation
(*81*)

Divine revelation is transmitted "to the successors of the apostles so that, enlightened by the Spirit of truth, they may faithfully preserve, expound and spread it abroad by their preaching."

> *I felt I had to write and urge you to contend for the faith that was once for all entrusted to the saints (Jude 3).*
> *In the past God spoke to our forefathers through the prophets at many times and in various ways, but in these last*

days he has spoken to us by his Son, whom he appointed heir of all things, and through whom he made the universe (Hebrews 1:1–2).

Assumption of Mary's Body into Heaven
(966)

"The assumption of the Blessed Virgin is a singular participation in her Son's Resurrection and an anticipation of the resurrection of other Christians: In giving birth you kept your virginity; in your Dormition you did not leave the world, O Mother of God, but were joined to the source of Life. You conceived the living God and, by your prayers, will deliver our souls from death."

> *But Christ has indeed been raised from the dead, the first fruits of those who have fallen asleep...But each in his own turn: Christ, the first fruits; then, when he comes, those who belong to him (1 Corinthians 15:20, 23).*

Baptism, Infant
(1250)

"The Church and the parents would deny a child the grace of *becoming a child of God* were they not to confer baptism shortly after birth."

> *Yet to all who received him, to those who believed in his name, he gave the right to become children of God—children born not of natural descent, nor of human decision or a husband's will, but born of God (John 1:12–13).*

Baptism (Water) Regenerates through the Holy Spirit
(1213)

"Through baptism we are freed from sin and reborn as sons of God; we become members of Christ, are incorporated into the Church and made sharers in her mission: baptism is the sacrament of regeneration through water in the word."

> *Can anyone keep these people from being baptized with water? They have received the Holy Spirit just as we have (Acts 10:47).*

Celibacy of Clergy
(1579)

"All ordained ministers…intend to remain celibate for the sake of the kingdom of heaven."

> *Don't we have the right to take a believing wife along with us, as do the other apostles and the Lord's brothers and Cephas (1 Corinthians 9:5)? See also Matthew 8:14.*

Holy Days of Obligation
(2192)

"On Sundays and other holy days of obligation the faithful are bound to participate in the Mass."

> *How is it that you are turning back to those weak and miserable principles? Do you wish to be enslaved by them all over again? You are observing special days and months and seasons and years! I fear for you, that somehow I have wasted my efforts on you (Galatians 4:9–11).*

Immaculate Conception of Mary
(491)

"The most Blessed Virgin Mary was from the first moment of her conception…preserved immune from all stain of original sin."

> *Therefore, just as sin entered the world through one man, and death through sin, and in this way death came to all men, because all sinned (Romans 5:12).*

> *For all have sinned and fall short of the glory of God (Romans 3:23).*

Indulgences
(1471–79)

"Since the faithful departed now being purified are also members of the same communion of saints, one way we can help them is to obtain indulgences for them, so that the temporal punishments due for their sins may be remitted."

> *No man can redeem the life of another or give to God a ransom for him…the ransom for a life is costly, no payment is ever enough (Psalm 49:7–8).*

> *When Simon (the Sorcerer) saw that the Spirit was given at the laying on of the apostles' hands, he offered them money and said, "Give me also this ability so that everyone on whom I lay my hands may receive the Holy Spirit." Peter answered: "May your money perish with you, because you thought you could buy the gift of God with money! You have no part or share in this ministry, because your heart is not right before God. Repent of this wickedness and pray to the Lord. Perhaps he will forgive you for having such a thought in your heart. For I see that you are full of bitterness and captive to sin" (Acts 8:18–23).*

Justification by Faith plus Works
(Trent, Sixth Session, Canon 9)

"If anyone says that the sinner is justified by faith alone, meaning that nothing else is required to cooperate in order to obtain the grace of justification…let him be anathema."

> *(Sinners) are justified freely by his grace through the redemption that came by Christ Jesus. God presented him as a sacrifice of atonement, through faith in his blood. He did this to demonstrate his justice, because in his forbearance he had left the sins committed beforehand unpunished…he did it to demonstrate his justice at the present time, so as to be just and the one who justifies those who have faith in Je-*

sus...For we maintain that a man is justified by faith apart from observing the law (Romans 3:24–26, 28).

However, to the man who does not work but trusts God who justifies the wicked, his faith is credited as righteousness (Romans 4:5).

Magisterium as the sole interpreter of the Word of God
(100)

"The task of interpreting the Word of God authentically has been entrusted solely to the Magisterium of the Church, that is, to the Pope and to the bishops in communion with him."

We do not use deception, nor do we distort the word of God. On the contrary, by setting forth the truth plainly we commend ourselves to every man's conscience in the sight of God (2 Corinthians 4:2).

As for you, the anointing you received from him remains in you, and you do not need anyone to teach you. But as his anointing teaches you about all things and as that anointing is real, not counterfeit (1 John 2:27). See also Proverbs 3:5–6.

Mary exalted as the Mediatrix of saving Grace
(969)

"Taken up to heaven she did not lay aside this saving office but by her manifold intercession continues to bring us the gifts of eternal salvation. ...Therefore the Blessed Virgin is invoked in the Church under the titles of Advocate, Helper, Benefactress, and Mediatrix."

For there is one God and one mediator between God and men, the man Christ Jesus (1 Timothy 2:5).

As Jesus was saying these things, a woman in the crowd called out, "Blessed is the mother who gave you birth and nursed you." He replied, "Blessed rather are those who hear the word of God and obey it" (Luke 11:27–28).

Meriting grace through good works
(2027)

"Moved by the Holy Spirit, we can merit for ourselves and for others <u>all</u> the graces needed to attain eternal life."

And if by grace, then it is no longer by works; if it were, grace would no longer be grace (Romans 11:6).

Papal Infallibility
(890)

"Christ endowed the Church's shepherds with the chrism of infallibility in matters of faith and morals."

When Peter came to Antioch, I opposed him to his face, because he was clearly in the wrong. Before certain men came from James, he used to eat with the Gentiles. But when they arrived, he began to draw back and separate himself from the Gentiles because he was afraid of those who belonged to the circumcision group. The other Jews joined him in his hypocrisy, so that by their hypocrisy even Barnabas was led astray. They were not acting in line with the truth of the gospel (Galatians 2:11–14).

Peter the Rock on which the Church is built
(552)

"Because of the faith he confessed Peter will remain the un-shakable rock of the Church."

The church is "built on the foundation of the apostles and prophets, with Christ Jesus himself as the chief cornerstone" (Ephesians 2:20).

Pope as Head of the Church
(882)

"For the Roman Pontiff, by reason of his office as Vicar of Christ, and as pastor of the entire Church has full, supreme, and universal power over the whole Church, a power which he can always exercise unhindered."

And he (Jesus) is the head of the body, the church; he is the beginning and the firstborn from among the dead, so that in everything he might have the supremacy. Christ is the head over every power and authority (Colossians 1:18–20).

Prayers for the Dead
(1479)

"Since the faithful departed now being purified are also members of the same communion of saints, one way we can help them is to obtain indulgences for them, so that the temporal punishments due for their sins may be remitted."

Just as man is destined to die once, and after that to face judgment (Hebrews 9:27).

Prayers to the Dead
(2677)

"By asking Mary to pray for us, we acknowledge ourselves to be poor sinners and we address ourselves to the 'Mother of Mercy,' the All-Holy One. We give ourselves over to her now, in the Today of our lives. And our trust broadens further, already at the present moment, to surrender 'the hour of our death' wholly to her care."

Let no one be found among you who…is a medium or spiritist or who consults the dead. Anyone who does these things is detestable to the LORD (Deuteronomy 18:10–12).

Priests Offering Sacrifices for Sin
(1369, 1414)

"Through the ministry of priests the spiritual sacrifice of the faithful is completed in union with the sacrifice of Christ the only Mediator, which in the Eucharist is offered through the priests' hands in the name of the whole Church in an unbloody and sacramental manner until the Lord himself comes. As a sacrifice, the Eucharist is also offered in reparation for the sins of the living and the dead."

Nowhere in the New Testament do you find priests offering sacrifices for sin.

> When this priest (Jesus) had offered for all time one sacrifice for sins, he sat down at the right hand of God (Hebrews 10:12).

> And where these (sins) have been forgiven, there is no longer any sacrifice for sin (Hebrews 10:18). See also John 19:30.

Purgatory to Purify Sins
(1030)

"All who die in God's grace and friendship, but still imperfectly purified, are indeed assured of their eternal salvation; but after death they undergo purification, so as to achieve the holiness necessary to enter the joy of heaven."

> After He had provided purification for sins, he sat down at the right hand of the Majesty in heaven. (Hebrews 1:3)

> The blood of Jesus, his Son, _purifies_ us from all sin (1 John 1:7).

> We have been made _holy_ through the sacrifice of the body of Jesus Christ once for all…by one sacrifice he has made _perfect forever_ those who are being made holy (Hebrews 10:10, 14).

Rosary
(971)

"The Church's devotion to the Blessed Virgin is intrinsic to Christian worship…the rosary, an 'epitome of the whole Gospel,' express this devotion to the Virgin Mary."

And when you pray, do not keep on babbling like pagans, for they think they will be heard because of their many words (Matthew 6:7).

Second Commandment Removed
(2142)

The Catholic Catechism has removed the second commandment given to Moses in Exodus 20:4–5. They still come up with a total of ten by dividing the tenth commandment into two.

You shall not make for yourself an idol in the form of anything in heaven above or on the earth beneath or in the waters below. You shall not bow down to them or worship them; for I, the LORD your God, am a jealous God (Exodus 20:4–5).

Statues, Crucifixes, Images, Icons
(1161)

"Following the divinely inspired teaching of our holy Fathers and the tradition of the Catholic Church (for we know that this tradition comes from the Holy Spirit who dwells in her) we rightly define with full certainty and correctness that, like the figure of the precious and life-giving cross, venerable and holy images of our Lord and God and Savior, Jesus Christ, our inviolate Lady, the holy Mother of God, and the venerated angels, all the saints and the just, whether painted or made of mosaic or another suitable material, are to be exhibited in the holy churches of God, on sacred vessels and vestments, walls and panels, in houses and on streets."

In addition to disobeying the second commandment of God in Exodus 20:4–5, there are other Scriptures that speak against this practice.

Although they claimed to be wise, they became fools and ex-changed the glory of the immortal God for images made to look like mortal man. They exchanged the truth of God for a lie, and worshipped and served created things rather than the Creator who is forever praised (Romans 1:22, 23, 25). See also Deuteronomy 27:15; 1 John 5:21; Revelation 9:20; 2 Corinthians 6:16.

The Mass as the Reappearance of Christ to be Worshipped and Sacrificed
(1367, 1377)

"The sacrifice of Christ and the sacrifice of the Eucharist are one single sacrifice: In this divine sacrifice which is celebrated in the Mass, the same Christ who offered himself once in a bloody manner on the altar of the cross is contained and is offered in an unbloody manner." Worship of the Eucharist is expressed by "genuflecting or bowing deeply as a sign of adoration of the Lord."

> *But now he has appeared once for all at the end of the ages to do away with sin by the sacrifice of himself (Hebrews 9:26).*

Transubstantiation—Bread and Wine Becomes Jesus
(1413)

"Under the consecrated species of bread and wine Christ himself, living and glorious, is present in a true, real, and substantial manner: his Body and his Blood, with his soul and his divinity."

> *This tradition is built on a literal translation of John 6:29-69, yet Jesus says in verse 63 that the words are spiritual. If anyone says to you, "Look, here is the Christ!" or, "There he is!" do not believe it…For as lightning that comes from the east is visible even in the west, so will be the coming of the Son of Man. (Matthew 24:23, 27)*

> *This same Jesus, who has been taken from you into heaven, will come back in the same way you have seen him go into heaven" (Acts 1:11).*

Venial Sins
(1863)

"Venial sin does not set us in direct opposition to the will and friendship of God; it does not break the covenant with God."

For whoever keeps the whole law and yet stumbles at just one point is guilty of breaking all of it (James 2:10).
The soul who sins is the one who will die (Ezekiel 18:4).
The wages of sin is death (Romans 6:23).

Summary

The evidence is overwhelming. Clearly it is impossible to believe both the Word of God and the teachings and traditions of the Roman Catholic Church. God has revealed His truth through His written Word, not the traditions of men. We must trust and obey the Sovereign Lord, for our destiny is in His hands, not in the hands of the Catholic clergy. Remember, "faith comes from hearing the message, and the message is heard through the *word of Christ*" (Romans 10:17). We are "born again, not of perishable seed, but of imperishable, through the *living and enduring word of God*" (1 Peter 1:23). The Apostle Paul, wrote, "By this gospel you are saved, if you hold firmly to the word I preached to you. Otherwise, you have believed in vain. For what I received I passed on to you as of first importance: that Christ died for our sins *according to the Scriptures*, that he was buried, that he was raised on the third day *according to the Scriptures* (1 Corinthians 15:2–4). Notice the gospel is according to the Scriptures, not tradition. Over and over again, throughout the Bible, we see the importance of believing the Scriptures and not the traditions of men. The holy Scriptures *are able* to make you wise for salvation through faith in Christ Jesus (2 Timothy 3:15). The Scriptures are sufficient to teach us God's wonderful gospel of salvation. We need nothing else. We need none of man's traditions and we need no other books.

13

A Catholic vs. a Christian

Roman Catholics are quick to make a distinction between their faith and the faith of those who call themselves Christians. We would agree that there is indeed some important differences. By definition we propose a Christian is one who has repented and believed the Gospel, while a Catholic is one who has been baptized and believes the teachings and traditions of his/her church. Some would say Roman Catholicism is a Christian denomination. Others, who know Roman Catholicism, would say it is not. They give two reasons for their position: 1) the Roman Catholic teaching on salvation contradicts the biblical teaching of salvation, and 2) it is impossible for anyone to believe two opposing views simultaneously. We recognize there are some Christians who may be attending the Catholic Church, but if they have repented and believed the Gospel they are no longer Catholics. The Holy Spirit will eventually lead them out to worship God in Spirit and Truth (John 4:24). Following is an objective contrast between the opposing beliefs of Catholics and Bible-believing Christians. (Official Catholic teaching is presented in parenthesis by paragraph number from the Catechism of the Catholic Church.)

Authority

A Christian believes Scripture has authority over the church.

All Scripture is God-breathed and is useful for teaching, rebuking, correcting and training in righteousness. (2 Timothy 3:16).

By setting forth the truth plainly we commend ourselves to every man's conscience (2 Corinthians 4:2).

A Catholic believes the Church has authority over Scripture. The manner of interpreting Scripture is ultimately subject to the judgment of the Church, which exercises the divinely conferred commission and ministry of watching over and interpreting the Word of God (119).

Justification

A Christian is justified once by faith because justification is a permanent declaration by God (Romans 8:30).

However, to the man who does not work, but trusts God who justifies the wicked, his faith is credited as righteousness (Romans 4:5).

A Catholic must be justified repeatedly by sacraments and works after he loses the grace of justification through mortal sin. The sacrament of Penance offers a new possibility to convert and to recover the grace of justification (1446).

Regeneration

A Christian believes he is regenerated by the baptism of the Spirit.

For we were all baptized by one Spirit into one body (1 Corinthians 12:13).

From the beginning God chose you to be saved through the sanctifying work of the Spirit and through belief in the truth (2 Thessalonians 2:13).

A Catholic believes baptism of water imparts divine life; the water of baptism truly signifies our birth into the divine life (694).

Salvation

A Christian is saved by God's unmerited grace.

> *For it is by grace you have been saved, through faith—and this not from yourselves, it is the gift of God–not by works, so that no one can boast (Ephesians 2:8–9).*

A Catholic is saved by meriting the graces needed for salvation. "We can merit for ourselves and for others the graces needed for the attainment of eternal life" (2010).

Good Works

A Christian is saved for good works.

> *For we are God's workmanship, created in Christ Jesus to do good works, which God prepared in advance for us to do (Ephesians 2:10).*

A Catholic is saved by good works. The sacraments of the New Covenant are necessary for salvation (1129).

Duration of Salvation

A Christian is saved for all eternity.
> *You also were included in Christ when you heard the word of truth, the gospel of your salvation. Having believed, you were marked in him with a seal, the promised Holy Spirit, who is a deposit guaranteeing our inheritance. (Ephesians 1:13–14).*

A Catholic is saved until a mortal sin is committed. Those who die in a state of mortal sin descend into hell (1035).

Offer of Salvation

A Christian believes salvation is offered to those outside the church.

> *We are therefore Christ's ambassadors as though God were making His appeal through us (2 Corinthians 5:20).*

A Catholic believes salvation is offered through the Church. Basing itself on Scripture and Tradition, the Council teaches that the Church, a pilgrim now on earth, is necessary for salvation. Anyone refusing to enter it or remain in it cannot be saved (846).

Purification of Sin

A Christian is purified by blood.

> *The blood of Jesus…purifies us from all sin (1 John 1:7).*

A Catholic is purified by the fires of Purgatory. They undergo purification in Purgatory, so as to achieve the holiness necessary to enter the joy of heaven (1030–31).

Saints

A Christian becomes a saint when the Spirit baptizes him into the body of Christ.

> *And He gave some…for the equipping of the saints…the body of Christ (Ephesians 4:11–12).*

A Catholic becomes a saint only if canonized by the Pope. This occurs when he solemnly proclaims that they practiced heroic virtue and lived in fidelity to God's grace (828).

Priests

A Christian is a priest.

> *But you are a chosen people, a royal priesthood, a holy nation, a people belonging to God (1 Peter 2:9).*

A Catholic needs a priest. Catholic priests are said to be apostolic successors and guarantee that Christ is acting in the sacraments to dispense divine life (1120–1131).

The Lord's Supper

A Christian believes the Lord's Supper is a memorial.

Do this in remembrance of me (1 Corinthians 11:24–25).

A Catholic believes the Lord's Supper is a sacrifice. The sacrifice of Christ and the sacrifice of the Eucharist are one single sacrifice…the same Christ who offered Himself once in a bloody manner on the altar of the cross is contained and offered in an unbloody manner (1367).

How Jesus Is Received

A Christian receives Jesus once, spiritually, in the heart.

Yet to all who received him, to those who believed in his name, he gave the right to become children of God (John 1:12).

God…put his Spirit in our hearts as a guarantee (2 Corinthians 1:22).

A Catholic believes he receives Jesus physically, frequently, in the stomach. The body, blood…soul and divinity of our Lord Jesus Christ…is truly, really and substantially contained in the Eucharist (1374-78).

Condemnation

A Christian is condemned by the Roman Catholic Church. Over 100 anathemas against Christians have been pronounced by the Roman Catholic Councils of Trent and Vatican II. These condemnations can only be revoked if a Christian returns to the Catholic Church and submits to the authority of the pope.

A Catholic is condemned by the Word of God.

There is a judge for the one who rejects me and does not accept my words; that very word which I spoke will condemn him at the last day (John 12:48).

If we or an angel from heaven should preach a gospel other than the one we preached to you, let him be eternally condemned (Galatians 1:6–9)!

Summary

These thirteen teachings and traditions of Roman Catholicism demonstrate that a Catholic Christian is indeed an oxymoron. The truth must be made known. Catholics, who believe they are Christians, must be lovingly confronted with the truth.

God's Word is truth (John 17:17). It is objective, authoritative, and sufficient! We must use it to expose the evil deeds of darkness, to set captives free from the bondage of deception. The "father of lies" continues to seduce many by mixing a little error with truth. In the final analysis, truth mixed with error never hurts the error; it only contaminates the truth. The veneer of truth covering Rome's false gospel is deceiving not only Catholics but many Protestants as well. Let us all turn from the errors of man's teachings to the truth of God's Word!

14

The Apostolic vs. The Apostate Church

Is the Roman Catholic Church the one true church founded by Christ, or is it an apostate church that has departed from the faith of the apostles? This question had a very clear-cut answer 400 years ago when the Protestant Reformers departed from the traditional teachings of the popes. Today, however, there are many evangelicals on each side of the debate. There are numerous warnings in Scripture about false teachers and deceivers who would attempt to lead people away from the truth. Jude warned the church to contend for the faith against apostates who attempt to steal away disciples. In verse 4 of his epistle he wrote: "For certain men whose condemnation was written about long ago have secretly slipped in among you. They are godless men, who change the grace of our God into a license for immorality and deny Jesus Christ our only sovereign and Lord."

Jude identifies the apostates by certain characteristics. They are ungodly because they supplant God's sovereign authority with an authority of their own. Apostates turn the grace of God into a commodity that can be bought, bartered, or merited. They pervert the gospel of grace into a gospel of works. They deny the supremacy and sovereignty of Christ and give His divine attributes and titles to others. They deny the sufficiency of the Word and work of Christ. It is these impostors who lead people away from "the faith which was once for all delivered to the saints." Are these perversions prevalent or descriptive of the Roman Catholic Church? Let us compare what Jude said of apostates with teachings from the new *Catechism of the Catholic Church* (paragraph numbers are in parenthesis).

Apostates Teach a Different Gospel

The Catholic Church has nullified the gospel of grace by adding additional requirements for salvation. It teaches that baptism (1257), church membership (845), the sacraments (1129), obeying the commandments (2068), good works (1821), and the sacrifice of the mass (1405) are all necessary for salvation. This is another gospel, and those who teach it are condemned as severely as Paul condemned the Judaizers for teaching a false gospel (Galatians 1:6–9). Catholic priests are needed to dispense salvation through seven sacraments. From baptism through purgatory, Catholics are taught that they can gain a right standing before God by what they do instead of believing what God has done for them through Christ. Catholics are taught they "can merit the graces needed for the attainment of eternal life" (2027). Each Catholic must attain his or her own salvation (1477).

Apostates Deny Salvation on the Merits of Christ Alone

The Catholic Church teaches that through indulgences "Catholics can attain their own salvation and at the same time cooperate in saving their brothers" (1477). The pope claims to have the power to transfer the merits of one sinner to another to reduce their punishment for sin. "An indulgence is a remission of the temporal punishment due to sins which the sinner gains through the Church, which...dispenses from the Vatican treasury...the prayers and good works of Mary and all the saints" (1471-79). Rome also "commends alms-giving and works of penance undertaken on behalf of the dead" (1032). Yet from Scripture we know that "No man can redeem the life of another or give to God a ransom for him—the ransom for life is costly no payment is ever enough" (Psalm 49:7–8).

For over 400 years Rome has not only preached a different gospel, but also has condemned anyone who believes the glorious gospel of grace. Many Christians are unaware that the Councils of Trent and Vatican II issued over 100 anathemas (condemnations) on anyone who believes salvation is by grace alone through faith alone in Christ alone. All these condemnations are still in effect today as evidenced by these two examples:

> "If anyone says the sinner is justified by faith alone, meaning that nothing else is required to cooperate in order to obtain the grace of justification, let him be anathema." (Canon 9, 6th Session, Council of Trent)

> The Catholic Church "condemns with anathema those who say that indulgences are useless or that the Church does not have the power to grant them." (Vatican Council II, The Conciliar and Post Conciliar Documents, Austin Flannery, "Apostolic Constitution on the Revision of Indulgences," Chapter 4)

Rome also condemns anyone who believes that they are assured of eternal life. This anathema denies the words of Christ, who said, "I give them eternal life and they shall never perish; no one can snatch them out of my hand" (John 10:28). For those who reject the words of Christ, Jesus said, "there is a judge for the one who does not accept my words; that very word which I spoke will condemn him at the last day" (John 12:48). Catholics must recognize there are more serious consequences for being condemned by the infallible Word of God than by the fallible teachings of their church.

Apostates Deny the Sufficiency of Christ's Atonement

Catholic teaching denies that Christ's sacrifice was sufficient to expiate all the guilt and punishment of sin. Instead they teach a cleansing fire is needed for "those who are expiating their sins in purgatory" (1475). The doctrine of purgatory is an utter denial of the sufficiency of Christ's perfect sacrifice for sin, yet Catholics are asked to accept it as a grace (1473). The pope has the power to bring them out of purgatory, but refuses to do so unless indulgences are offered in their name. "All who die still imperfectly purified undergo purification, so as to achieve the holiness necessary to enter the joy of heaven." (1030).

Rome teaches that Catholics can carry their own cross to expiate their sins and the sins of others (1474-77). What a glaring contradiction this is. The cross of the sinless and perfect Savior is said to be insufficient to expiate sins, yet the cross of lowly sinners is said to be sufficient to do what Christ could not do. No priest can tell Catholics how many indulgences are needed or how long one has to suffer for each sin. This only perpetuates a religious system that holds Catholics in bondage and at the mercy of their church indefinitely. However the writer of Hebrews declared: "For by one offering He (Jesus) has perfected for all time those who are sanctified" (10:14), and "after Christ had provided purification for sins, He sat down at the right hand of the majesty in heaven" (1:3).

Apostates Deny Christ's Sacrifice is Finished

The Catholic Church teaches that the sacrifice of Jesus must continue daily on its altars for the reparation of the sins of the living and the dead (1414). This is done so that sins may be expiated and the wrath of God may be appeased. Although Scriptures teach the Lord's Supper is a memorial, Rome declares it is a real sacrifice and asserts that Jesus is immolated (killed) as a sacrificial victim each time the Mass is offered. "The sacrifice of Christ and the sacrifice of the Eucharist are one single sacrifice" (1367). Rome claims the priest has the power to call Jesus down from heaven, and transubstantiate a wafer into His physical body, blood, soul, and divinity. After almighty God has been reduced to a lifeless, inanimate piece of bread the priest lifts it up to be worshipped. The priest then once again presents Jesus Christ as a sacrifice to the Father. This practice is strongly rebuked by Scripture. Paul wrote: "we know that since Christ was raised from the dead, He cannot die again…the death He died He died to sin once for all" (Romans 6:9–10). In anticipation that apostates would declare Christ is present when He is not, Jesus warned us that if anyone says to you, "look here is the Christ, or there He is, do not believe it" (Matthew 24:23). When Jesus "offered for all time one sacrifice for sins, He sat down at the right hand of God…there is no longer any sacrifice for sin" (Hebrews 10:12, 18). To deny the words of our blood-stained Savior, who said, "It is finished," is to reject the essential doctrine of the gospel (John 19:31). For if the work of redemption is not finished, then all humanity remains condemned to hell and dead in their sins.

Apostates Deny the Sufficiency and Authority of God's Word

Rome declares that Scripture along with "tradition must be accepted and honored with equal sentiments of devotion and reverence" (*Catechism of the Catholic Church*, 82). Pagan traditions and practices began tainting the doctrinal purity of the early church when it ignored the rebuke of Jesus concerning tradition. Jesus firmly denounced religious leaders for allowing their traditions to nullify the Word of God (Mark 7:6–13). Apostates show a lack of awe and reverence of God's sovereign power by supplanting His authority with an authority of their own. They do this by removing, adding, and altering the inspired Word of God. Catholic Bishops have removed the 2nd commandment of God in their new Catechism (page 496). It is no wonder Rome removed the commandment, that forbids the making and worshipping of statues. There are huge profits that have been made from the sale of statues. In the 16th century Rome added the Apocrypha to its canon of inspired books in an attempt to justify its doctrine of Purgatory. Rome should take heed of the warnings God gives to those who add to His word: "Do not add to his words or he will rebuke you and prove you a liar" (Proverbs 30:5–6).

Apostates Demand Submission to Mediators Other than Christ

Catholics must submit to the pope who "by reason of his office as Vicar of Christ has full supreme and universal power over the whole church, a power he can exercise unhindered" (882). They must also submit to The Magisterium, which is said to be the infallible teaching authority of the Church. Catholics are taught that they cannot receive forgiveness for mortal sins unless they confess them to yet another mediator, a priest. Catholics also seek Mary as a mediator who has been elevated to mediatrix, co-redeemer, and advocate by Rome. Yet Scripture reveals Jesus is the only mediator between God and man (1 Timothy 2:5). Jesus alone is holy, blameless, pure, set apart from sinners, and exalted above the heavens (Hebrews 7:26).

Is the Roman Catholic Church guilty of apostasy? The evidence appears to be overwhelming. The truth must be told in love with courage and conviction. The eternal destiny of millions of precious souls hangs in the balance. The Catholic Church has fallen away from the faith of the apostles and gone the way of apostates.

How are Christians to respond? Toward individual Catholics we must obey the Scriptures and call them out of their apostate churches (Revelation 18:4). We must proclaim the true gospel and make disciples of them! Toward the religious system that holds Catholics in bondage we must expose their unfruitful deeds of darkness (Ephesians 5:11). We must correct and rebuke their false teaching (2 Timothy 4:2) and contend for the faith (Jude 3). And finally we must avoid those who oppose sound doctrine (Romans 16:17). This means refusing to join hands with apostates "to advance the mission of Christ." It means rebuking the ecumenical thrust for unity at the expense of truth. We must obey the Scriptures for the glory and purpose of Christ. May He be exalted and praised in all that we do!

15

The Sacrifice of the Mass: Blessing or Bondage?

Many former Catholics have looked back on their experience of going to church for Mass as a prison sentence, something they had to do in order to avoid the penalty of a mortal sin. Others remember it as a mindless ritual of standing, sitting, kneeling, and reciting as the priest performed his religious duties. All Catholics are obligated by the laws of their church to attend church every week: "On Sundays and other holy days of obligation the faithful are bound to participate in the Mass" (paragraph 2180 of the *Catechism of the Catholic Church*). With this law so explicit and demanding, the question that begs an answer is: Why is participation so compulsory for Catholics? The answers are complex, controversial, and authoritative. They are found in the *Catechism of the Catholic Church* and are noted by paragraph numbers in parenthesis. First let us look to the Catechism to define the Mass and the Eucharist:

> The Mass is…the sacrificial memorial in which the sacrifice of the cross is perpetuated (1382). The Eucharist is thus a sacrifice because it represents (makes present) the sacrifice of the cross…and because it applies its fruit… the forgiveness of the sins we daily commit. The sacrifice of Christ and the sacrifice of the Eucharist are one single sacrifice: The victim is one and the same. In this divine sacrifice which is celebrated in the Mass, the same Christ

who offered himself once in a bloody manner on the altar of the cross is contained and is offered in an unbloody manner (1366, 1367).

Catholics are given no choice but to believe these inconceivable teachings. Is the Lord Jesus really physically present in the Eucharist? How Catholics answer this question has serious consequences. If they deny the presence of Jesus they are condemned by their church. Canon 1 of the Council of Trent:

> If anyone denies, that in the sacrament of the most Holy Eucharist, are contained truly, really and substantially the body and blood together with the soul and divinity of our Lord Jesus Christ, and consequently the whole Christ...let him be anathema.

Conversely, if they worship the Eucharist as the Lord Jesus, they commit the sin of idolatry, a sin similar to the sin of the Israelites who worshipped a golden calf as their God. Those who committed this sin suffered the wrath of almighty God (Exodus 32:1–28).

Catholics are taught that their redemption comes not from the perfect and finished sacrifice of Jesus on Calvary's cross, but through the ongoing repetitious liturgy of the Mass. "For it is in the liturgy, especially in the divine sacrifice of the Eucharist, that the work of our redemption is accomplished. Every time this mystery is celebrated, the work of our redemption is carried on" (1068, 1405). "In the liturgy of the Mass we express our faith in the real presence of Christ by genuflecting or bowing deeply as a sign of adoration of the Lord" (1374, 1378). The Church knows that "the Lord comes even now in his Eucharist and that he is there in our midst" (1404).

Clearly the Roman Catholic Church teaches the Lord Jesus Christ returns to the earth every day to be worshipped and sacrificed. But how can this be? We know Jesus must return physically to the earth in the same way in which He departed (not in the form of a wafer): "This Jesus, who has been taken up from you into heaven, will come in just the same way as you have watched Him go into heaven" (Acts 1:11). We also know, from the prophet Zechariah, that when Jesus comes back He will return to the Mt. of Olives (14:4). Jesus described how and when He would return to the earth. He said, "For just as the lightning comes from the east, and flashes even to the west, so shall the coming of the Son of Man be...immediately after the tribulation...and then all the tribes of the earth will mourn, and they will see the Son of Man coming on the clouds of the sky with power and great glory" (Matthew 24:27–30).

Yet Catholic priest John O'Brien rejects God's Word concerning the details of Christ's return in his book, *The Faith of Millions*:

> When the priest announces the tremendous words of consecration, he reaches up into the heavens, brings Christ down from His throne, and places Him upon our altar to be offered up again as the Victim for the sins of man. It is a power greater than that of saints and angels, greater than that of Seraphim and Cherubim. The priest brings Christ down from heaven, and renders Him present on our altar as the eternal Victim for the sins of man, not once but a thousand times! The priest speaks and lo! Christ, the eternal and omnipotent God, bows his head in humble obedience to the priest's command.

As preposterous and unthinkable as this may sound, the Catholic priest is said to have the power to call almighty God down from heaven and then continue to do what the Lord Jesus declared He had finished. Over 200,000 times each day, on Catholic altars throughout the world, priests believe they represent Jesus as a sacrificial victim for sins. The Lord Jesus endured excruciating pain and torture for sinners once for all time. "He was pierced through for our transgressions and crushed for our iniquities" (Isaiah 53:5). It is unconscionable that Catholics would want to continue His suffering on their altars. Not only does Rome purport to continue this horrific sacrifice with Jesus as its "victim," it dares to say that this sacrifice has power to forgive sin:

> The Eucharist is also offered in reparation for the sins of the living and the dead and to obtain spiritual or temporal benefits from God. Holy Communion separates us from sin. I should always receive it, so that it may always forgive my sins. Because I always sin, I should always have a remedy (1393, 1414).

What absurdity! The perfect and actual sacrifice of Jesus, who poured out genuine blood and died a real death, is said to be insufficient to forgive all sins, but its blasphemous representation on Catholic altars is said to have the power to forgive the sins that Jesus failed to expiate. Yes, the Catholic Mass blatantly denies the sufficiency of Christ's atonement that is so clearly stated in Scripture. In the book of Hebrews we read that the believer's redemption is secure and the work is finished because of one perfect offering for sin. "By His (Christ's) own blood He entered in once into the holy place, having obtained eternal redemption for us" (9:12). We also read: "So Christ was once (not many times) offered to bear the sins of many" (9:28). Again, "we are sanctified through the offering of the body of Jesus Christ once (no representations) for all" (10:10). Continuing, "But this Man (Jesus) after He had offered one sacrifice for sins forever, sat down on the right hand of God... For by one offering (not many) He has perfected forever them that are sanctified" (10:12, 14). We also read: "there is no more offering for sin" (10:18).

God's promises revealed in the gospel are null and void to those who teach and believe the doctrine of the Mass. Those poor victims who faithfully participate in the Mass throughout their lives are not offered the peace of heaven on their deathbed, but the fires of purgatory. Once they die, purgatory demands more Masses to get them out, and so the deception and bondage of the Roman Catholic religion is perpetuated.

The sacrifice of the Mass more closely resembles the Old Testament animal sacrifices that had to be repeated and could never take away sins. By representing Jesus as a sacrificial "victim" in the Mass, the Catholic Church keeps Him cursed on the cross and forsaken by God instead of glorified at His Father's right hand. Catholic priests have attempted to rob Jesus Christ of His High Priestly office of intercession by assuming that responsibility themselves. Yet their roles as priests are spurious and fraudulent. The only true priesthood on earth that is recognized in the New Testament is the spiritual priesthood of all believers (1 Peter 2:9).

When the doctrine and practice of the Mass is tested against the Word of God, the only standard for measuring truth, we find definite and conclusive misinterpretations, errors, fallacies and heresies:

1. Jesus was never a "victim" as Rome purports, but went to the cross willingly in humble obedience to His Father (Philippians 2:8).

2. When Jesus said we must eat His flesh and drink His blood, His words were spiritual and not to be taken literally (John. 6:63). He was using figurative language, as He often did (John 16:25). His disciples were familiar with the figurative phrase "eating and drinking" to describe the appropriation of divine blessings to one's innermost being (Jeremiah 15:16; Isaiah 55:1–3).

3. Those who take "eating and drinking" literally must become cannibals to gain eternal life. Furthermore, consuming blood was forbidden; those who did were to be cut off. Jesus would not have asked the Jews to break the law (Leviticus 17:10–

14). This also presents a dilemma, "What if a person eats and drinks but does not believe?" Or "what if a person believes but does not eat and drink?"

4. The alleged change of bread and wine into flesh and blood is not a miracle, but a hoax because there is no change in appearance, substance, and taste. True biblical miracles were real and observable.

5. Rome says the Mass is a bloodless sacrifice, but a sacrifice without blood cannot atone for sins (Leviticus 17:11; Hebrews 9:22). Jesus instituted the Lord's Supper as a memorial not a sacrifice (Luke 22:19; 1 Corinthians 11:24)

6. Nowhere in the New Testament do we find priests offering sacrifices for sin or Masses for the dead. Catholic priests violate Christ's unique role as mediator between God and men. (1 Timothy 2:5).

7. To worship the elements of the Mass is to commit the sin of idolatry (Exodus 20:4-5).

The sacrifice of the Mass clearly violates God's Word and is a powerful deception that holds Catholics in bondage. All who fear God must come out and not participate in the sin of idolatry any longer. Mindful of Paul's sermon in Acts 17:23–30, I exhort all Catholics with similar words: What you worship in ignorance, this I proclaim to you: "The God who is Lord of heaven and earth, does not dwell in tabernacles made with hands; neither is He offered with human hands. The Divine Nature is not like flour and water, an image formed by the thought of man. God is now declaring men everywhere to repent."

16

Eucharistic Devotion: Worship or Idolatry?

Eucharistic adoration has increased dramatically in Roman Catholic churches throughout America due to the urging of the pope. Chapels have been set up in churches where Catholics can worship the real presence of Jesus. Some chapels offer Perpetual Eucharistic Adoration whereby the consecrated host is exposed and adored in a monstrance without interruption 24 hours a day, 7 days a week. Parishioners commit themselves to a specific day and time (one hour) every week. When they look upon the Sacred Host, they believe they are looking upon Jesus, the almighty God, who created heaven and earth.

The monstrance is a silver or gold stand with rays depicting a sun burst and a circular window where the Eucharist is placed. It comes from the Latin word "monstrare," to show or to expose to view. They vary in sizes, but one of the largest is the Monstrance of Toledo, Spain. It measures over 8 feet, has 15 kilos of pure gold, 183 kg. of silver, many precious jewels, and 260 small statues. The total weight is 218 kg.

Benefits of Adoring the Eucharist

Pope Pius XI associated the worship of Christ in The Blessed Sacrament with expiation for sin. The angel at Fatima and the Blessed Mother taught us to adore the Blessed Sacrament and make reparation for our sins. Pope Paul VI proclaimed, "How great is the value of conversation with Christ in the Blessed Sacrament, for there is nothing more efficacious for advancing along the road of holiness!" (*Mysterium Fidei*). John Paul II said that "all the evils of the world could be overcome through the great power of Perpetual Eucharistic Adoration. The devil is put to flight wherever Jesus is adored in the Most Blessed Sacrament." He asked, "How will young people be able to know the Lord if they are not introduced to the mystery of his pres-ence?" (*Lumen Gentium*). Catholics can now enjoy these benefits by adoring the Eucharist on the internet. A site using the technology of a "webcam" has been set up for this purpose.

Catholics view transubstantiation as the greatest of all miracles. Almighty God, who once humbled Himself to become man, now transforms Himself into lifeless, inanimate wafers. According to the 1994 Catechism of the Catholic Church, paragraphs 1374–1378, "The body and blood...soul and divinity of our Lord Jesus Christ...is truly, really, and substantially contained" in the Eucharist. Since each Eucharist contains the whole Christ, and since upwards of hundreds of wafers are consecrated during each mass, hundreds of Jesus Christs become physically present. Although the Vatican would never acknowledge it, this is a form of polytheism, the worship of many gods.

God Is Worshipped In Spirit

Jesus said, "God is spirit, and those who worship Him must worship in spirit [which is invisible] and truth" (John 4:24). After Jesus ascended into heaven, Paul said true worshippers are those "who worship in the Spirit of God" (Philippians 3:3). The eternal, immortal King is invisible to those on earth until He returns (1 Timothy 1:17). Christians are called to look on "the things which are not seen; for the things which are seen are temporal, but the things which are not seen are eternal" (2 Corinthians 4:18). The Eucharistic god of the Catholic Church is thus a temporal god and a false Christ. Jesus warned us not to believe anyone who says, "Here is the Christ" (Matthew 24:23). Jesus Christ, the Eternal God, is now physically present at the right hand of the Father (Luke 22:69). He will not return to the earth until after the tribulation (Matthew 24:29–30). Clearly, the worship of the Eucharist is idolatry. To worship any image in the place of God provokes Him to anger. God has this to say to idolaters: "They have made Me jealous with what is not God; they have provoked Me to anger with their idols" (Deuteronomy 32:21). The Roman Catholic Church has "exchanged the glory of the incorruptible God for an image" and "exchanged the truth of God for a lie" (Romans 1:23–25).

To teach that the incorruptible, almighty and holy God is contained in a corruptible wafer that can be handled, eaten, digested, and expelled is indeed the most irreverent, desecrating, and profane form of idolatry. When Isaiah was confronted with God's holiness he cried out, "Woe is me, I am undone. I am a man of unclean lips" (Isaiah 6:5). When asked what happens to Jesus after the Eucharist is consumed, priests try to explain the unexplainable by suggesting the body and blood, soul and divinity of Jesus departs from the Eucharist as it is being digested.

Idolatry's Punishment Is Death

Worshipping the Eucharist is a violation of the 2nd commandment:

> *"You shall not make for yourself an idol, or any likeness of what is in heaven above or on the earth beneath or in the water under the earth. You shall not worship them or serve them; for I, the Lord your God, am a jealous God"* (Exodus 20:1–5).

Catholics who worship the Eucharist can be closely compared to the Israelites who worshipped the golden calf as their true God (Exodus 32:4). Their punishment imposed by God for this most serious sin was death (Exodus 32:27–28).

God is too awesome and glorious to be captured in any image, let alone a wafer. The prophet Isaiah declares God's immeasurable greatness and then asks, "To whom then will you liken God? Or what likeness will you compare with Him" (Isaiah 40:18)? Any image of God is therefore an insult to His glorious holiness and majestic perfection.

Idolatry Is A Pagan Practice

From ancient times only pagan religions used images in the worship of their deities. This type of idolatry is just one of many pagan practices that crept into the Roman Catholic Church over time. Catholics must know that the Lord God does not dwell in the inner substance of a wafer, but in the very bodies of born-again Christians. The Apostle Paul asked: "What agreement has the temple of God with idols? For we are the temple of the living God; just as God said, 'I will dwell in them and walk among them; and I will be their God, and they shall be My people'" (2 Corinthians 6:16). Paul warned us that those who practice idolatry will not inherit the kingdom of God (Galatians 5:21).

What Should Roman Catholics Do?

"Flee from idolatry" (1 Corinthians 10:14). "Hear the Word of God and observe it" (Luke 11:28). Take heed of God's warnings! "Those who cling to worthless idols forfeit the grace that could be theirs" (Jonah 2:8, NIV). God's elect are commanded to come out of any religion that practices the sin of idolatry. "Come out of her, my people, that you may not participate in her sins" (Revelation 18:4). Those who remain will also participate in her punishment. Those who come out and turn to Jesus Christ, as He is so gloriously revealed in Scripture, will be set free. They will no longer be slaves to the Eucharist, that by nature is not God (Galatians 4:8). Roman Catholics must do as the Thessalonians did—turn from idols to serve the living and true God and wait for His Son from heaven (1 Thessalonians 1:9-10). May God help them to do so! And may Christians everywhere be moved with compassion to speak the truth in love to Roman Catholics, in the hopes of rescuing some from God's punishment.

17

Purgatory:
Purifying Fire or Fatal Fable

Catholics who believe that a purifying fire will purge away their sins are deluded victims of a fatal fabrication. The invention of a place for purification of sins called Purgatory is one of the most seductive attractions of the Roman Catholic religion. Pastor John MacArthur of Grace Community Church in Southern California described this deceptive hoax brilliantly:

> "Purgatory is what makes the whole system work. Take out Purgatory and it's a hard sell to be a Catholic. Purgatory is the safety net; when you die, you don't go to hell. You go [to Purgatory] and get things sorted out and finally get to heaven if you've been a good Catholic. In the Catholic system you can never know you're going to heaven. You just keep trying and trying…in a long journey toward perfection. Well, it's pretty discouraging. People in that system are guilt-ridden, fear-ridden, and have no knowledge of whether or not they're going to get into the Kingdom. If there's no Purgatory, there's no safety net to catch me and give me some opportunity to get into heaven. It's a second chance, it's another chance after death" (from the message "The Pope and the Papacy").

The Origin of Purgatory

There was no mention of Purgatory during the first two centuries of the church. However, when Roman Emperor Theodosius (379-395) decreed that Christianity was to be the official religion of the empire, thousands of pagans flooded into the Church and brought their pagan beliefs and traditions with them. One of those ancient pagan beliefs was a place of purification where souls went to make satisfaction for their sins.

The concept became much more widespread around A.D. 600 due to the fanaticism of Pope Gregory the Great. He developed the doctrine through visions and revelations of a Purgatorial fire. According to the *Catholic Encyclopedia* (CE), Pope Gregory said Catholics "will expiate their faults by purgatorial flames," and "the pain [is] more intolerable than any one can suffer in this life." Centuries later, at the Council of Florence (1431), it was pronounced to be an infallible dogma. It was later reaffirmed by the Council of Trent (1564). The dogma is based largely on Catholic tradition from extra-biblical writings and oral history. "So deep was this belief ingrained in our common humanity that it was accepted by the Jews, and in at least a shadowy way by the pagans, long before the coming of Christianity" (CE). It seems incomprehensible that Rome would admit to using a pagan tradition for the defense of one of its most esteemed "Christian" doctrines.

The Deception of Purgatory

Purgatory comes from the Latin word "purgare," which means to make clean or to purify. The *Catholic Encyclopedia* defines purgatory as "a place or condition of temporal punishment for those who, departing this life in God's grace, are not entirely free from venial faults, or have not fully paid the satisfaction due to their transgressions." They must be purified of these "venial" sins before they can be allowed into heaven. Here we see Catholicism perpetuating the seductive lie of Satan by declaring, as he did to Adam and Eve in Genesis 3:4, "you will not surely die" when you commit venial sins. The Council of Trent dares to declare that "God does not always remit the whole punishment due to sin together with the guilt. God requires satisfaction and will punish sin...The sinner, failing to do penance in this life, may be punished in another world, and so not be cast off eternally from God." (Session 15, Can. XI). Those Catholic bishops had the audacity to declare that the suffering and death of God's perfect man and man's perfect substitute was not sufficient to satisfy divine justice for sin.

The Motivation for Purgatory

Over the centuries billions of dollars have been paid to Roman Catholic priests to obtain relief from imaginary sufferings in Purgatory's fire. The Catholic clergy has always taught that the period of suffering in Purgatory can be shortened by purchasing indulgences and novenas, buying Mass cards, and providing gifts of money. When a Catholic dies, money is extracted from mourning loved ones to shorten the deceased's punishment in Purgatory. When my own dear dad passed away as a devout Catholic of 79 years, I was amazed at the hundreds of Mass cards purchased for him by well-meaning friends. We have heard of other Catholics who have willed their entire estates to their religion so that perpetual masses could be offered for them after they die. It is no wonder that the Catholic religion has become the richest institution in the world. The buying and selling of God's grace has been a very lucrative business for the Vatican.

Another motivation for Rome to fabricate the heretical doctrine of Purgatory is its powerful effect on controlling people. Ultimately the enslavement and subjugation of people is the goal of every false religion, and Purgatory does exactly that. The concept of a terrifying prison with a purging fire, governed by religious leaders, is a most brilliant invention. It holds people captive not only in this life, but also in the next life. Catholic clergy will not say how many years people have to suffer for their sins or how many Masses must be purchased before they can be released from the flames. This dreadful fear and uncertainty is the most ruthless form of religious bondage and deception!

Biblical Support for Purgatory

There is absolutely no Biblical support for the doctrine of Purgatory! In fact, neither the word nor the concept of sin-purifying fire is found in Scripture. The Vatican was confronted with this in the 16th century when the Reformers protested its practice of buying and selling God's grace through indulgences. Backed into a corner, the Council of Trent added the apocryphal books to its canon of Scripture. Rome now declares that there is scriptural support for purgatory in the apocryphal book of 2 Maccabees. The council ignored the fact that the Jewish scribes never recognized the apocryphal books as inspired or part of the Hebrew Scriptures. They were never included because of their many historical, theological, and geographical errors. Since God is not the author of error, He obviously did not inspire the writers of the Apocrypha. This is why the Apocrypha was never included in the original canon of 66 books.

The apocryphal verses Rome uses to defend its doctrine of Purgatory refer to Jewish soldiers who died wearing pagan amulets around their necks. Judas Maccabees "sent twelve thousand drachmas of silver to Jerusalem for sacrifice to be offered for the sins of the dead...Judas hoped that these men who died fighting for the cause of God and religion might find mercy, either because they might be excused from mortal sin by ignorance, or might have repented of their sin, at least at their death. It is therefore a holy and wholesome thought to pray for the dead, that they may be loosed from sins" (2 Maccabees 12:43–46). Rome argues that since Judas Maccabees prayed for the dead, there must be hope for those who die in sin. This, of course, goes directly against God's Word that declares: "It is appointed for men to die once and after this comes judgment" (Hebrews

9:22). Rome's attempt to give credence to Purgatory by using this ungodly practice of the Jews, who had a history of disobeying God, is pathetic.

In another attempt to find support for Purgatory, many Catholics point to this verse: "If any man's work is burned up, he will suffer loss; but he himself will be saved, yet so as through fire" (1 Corinthians 3:15). Clearly, the context of this verse is the testing of a man's works by fire. The works that survive are the ones done for the glory of Christ and are called gold, silver, and precious stones (1 Corinthians 3:12). All the other superfluous works are burned in fire and are called wood, hay, and stubble. It is not man's sins that are being purged, it is man's spurious works that are being burned and destroyed.

The Biblical Rebuke of Purgatory

God's Word leaves absolutely no possibility for sin to be purged away by anything other than the blood of Jesus Christ. The beloved Apostle John penned these words with irrefutable clarity. He wrote: "The blood of Jesus His Son cleanses us from all sin" and "all unrighteousness" (1 John 1:7, 9). John did not say "some" sins or "most" sins, but all sin! This soundly rebukes the need for a sin-purging fire. God's Word also declares: "All things are cleansed with blood, and without shedding of blood there is no forgiveness" (Hebrews 9:27). When Jesus "made purification of sins, He sat down at the right hand of the Majesty on high" (Hebrews 1:3). Those who desire to have their sins purged need to trust a person, not a place. The blood of Christ is the only cleansing agent for sin! Those who come to the cross of Christ must come with empty hands of faith, bringing nothing but their sins.

Every blood-bought believer is instantly present with their Redeemer at the moment of death. To be "absent from the body" is to be "at home with the Lord" (2 Corinthians 5:6–8). This good news was affirmed by the Lord Jesus with the promise He gave to the repentant thief at Calvary. He said to him, "Truly I say to you, today you shall be with Me in Paradise" (Luke 23:43). This habitual sinner did not need a fire to purge his sins.

Catholics who believe in Purgatory need to be asked: "Who is in charge of releasing souls from the purging fire?" It cannot be God because of His promise to believers. "Their sins and iniquities I will remember no more" (Hebrews 10:17). After conversion, God no longer counts sins against His children (2 Corinthians 5:19).

Purgatory is a travesty on the justice of God and a disgraceful fabrication that robs Christ Jesus of His glory and honor. He alone satisfied divine justice, once and for all, by the perfect and finished sacrifice of Himself. The fatal deception of Purgatory blinds Catholics from the glorious gospel of grace. It is one of Satan's many lies that keep his captives from knowing and trusting the sufficiency of Jesus Christ. It is Christ alone who will present us "faultless before the presence of His glory" (Jude 24).

18

Examine Yourselves: Are You in the Faith?

Many Catholics have an unyielding, strong, and impregnable faith. They stubbornly refuse to be swayed by any teaching that is not endorsed by their church. Even lapsed Catholics who have not been to church in years will come to the defense of their church whenever it is criticized. Most Catholics exhibit more trust and loyalty to their church than to Jesus. Is this the right kind of faith? From the Scriptures we see that there are two kinds of faith—"saving" faith, and "spurious" faith that leaves its adherents condemned in their sins. When we compare Roman Catholicism to Scripture we see two gospels preached, two roads to eternity, with only two destinations. The inescapable question for anyone is: "How can I know if I have true faith and have believed the true gospel?"

The Apostle Paul provides the answer in his epistles and with an exhortation: "Test yourselves to see if you are in the faith; examine yourselves (2 Corinthians 13:5)! Paul penned those words because many false teachers had been leading people away from "the faith" that was once for all delivered to the saints (Jude 3). In Paul's first letter to the Corinthians he pleaded with them to be aware of false teachers who were perverting the faith, the very gospel that he preached to them, and that they received, and in which they stood. Paul warned them they must hold fast to the word he preached, otherwise they would have believed in vain (1 Corinthians 15:1–4).

The Source and Object of Faith

How are we to test ourselves? What tests can we employ to see if our faith is genuine or spurious? First, we can examine the source and object of our faith. If faith is genuine its exclusive source must be the Word of God (Romans 10:17). This type of faith forsakes any and all teaching that does not conform to Scripture (2 Timothy 3:15–16). If faith is genuine, the exclusive object must be the Lord Jesus Christ, the eternal Son of God, who sovereignly secured the salvation of His people. He satisfied all the demands of God's holy law, then laid His life down as a substitute for sinners who come to Him with empty hands of faith. To trust the Lord Jesus for salvation is to forsake all other efforts, means, and mediators to save oneself (Acts 4:12).

The faith of Catholics rarely passes these two critical tests. More often than not they have the wrong sources. The Catholic faith relies heavily on extrabiblical sources such as Catechisms, new papal revelations, apparitions, early church fathers, or man-made traditions that are inconsistent with the eternal and resolutely unchangeable gospel. The object of most Catholics' faith is not Jesus alone. In fact, Jesus is seldom mentioned when Catholics are asked how they hope to get to heaven. Catholics, to a greater extent, trust their church and priests to dispense all the graces needed for salvation. Seldom is their faith "alone" because good works, sacraments, and inherent righteousness are necessary for Catholic salvation.

Indicators of Spurious Faith

Other indicators of spurious faith are evident whenever people: (1) desire Christ only as a Priest to procure pardon and peace, but not as a Prophet to instruct them or as a King to rule over them; (2) desire to be saved from the punishment of sin, but not from sin itself; (3) desire the blessings of Christ, but not a relationship with Him; and (4) reject many of Christ's promises because they go against their traditions.

Examples of Non-saving Faith

The New Testament gives several examples of non-saving faith. Jesus told us about temporary faith (Matthew 13:19). James wrote about dead faith (James 2:17). Paul warned against believing in vain (1 Corinthians 15:2). Simon the Sorcerer believed and was even baptized, but for the wrong motivation. He attempted to buy the grace of God in order to obtain miraculous power (Acts 8:9–24). Surely the most vivid example of spurious faith was given in the Sermon on the Mount. It is here that the most sobering words any professing Christian could ever hear are pronounced by Jesus: "I never knew you; depart from Me, you who practice lawlessness." Jesus doesn't say these words to pagans, Muslims, or Hindus, but to professing Christians who prophesied, cast out demons, and performed miracles in His Name (Matthew 7:21–23). How terrifying it will be for Catholics, who thought they were receiving Jesus through the Eucharist, to hear that He never knew them. How horrifying it will be for those who were baptized into a counterfeit Christianity to meet the Lord Jesus at the judgment instead of the wedding feast of the Lamb.

Another Jesus and Gospel

Believing another gospel and trusting another Jesus exhibits a spurious or false faith (2 Corinthians 11:4). The exclusivity of God's gospel will not allow a person to be saved while believing another gospel. Catholics fabricate another gospel because they trust a Jesus who is not the Jesus of Scripture. The Catholic Jesus never finished the work of redemption. Instead this false Christ is immolated on Catholic altars over 200,000 times each day. Catholics rely on purgatory and indulgences to purify and pay the punishment for sins because their Jesus did not save them completely. Whenever another Jesus is proclaimed, another gospel is needed to atone for whatever the counterfeit left undone.

False Teachers Block the Way

Here we see how great and powerful Satan and his instruments of deception are as they block the only door that leads to life (John 10:9). They are full of deceit and fraud, enemies of all righteousness, and never cease to make crooked the straight ways of the Lord (Acts 13:10). Priests who preach another Jesus point people away from the narrow door that leads to life. Jesus said, "Strive to enter by the narrow door; for many, I tell you, will seek to enter and will not be able" (Luke 13:24). The Greek word for strive is "agonizomai" which means to wrestle, to make every effort to achieve the goal. The word implies that there will be hindrances or obstacles to overcome. All who desire to know Jesus must strive in their search and not be carried about by every wind of doctrine, by the trickery of men, by craftiness in deceitful scheming (Ephesians 4:14). They must diligently search the Scriptures and rely on the supernatural power of the Holy Spirit to discern the true way from the counterfeit way (1 Corinthians 2:6–16). What a contrast this is to the *easy way of salvation* that the Vatican promotes. "Get baptized and you're born of God!" Paradoxically, it is the *easy way* of baptism that causes many to miss the true way—through faith alone in Jesus alone. The easy way becomes an obstacle sinners must overcome to enter the narrow door.

Baptismal regeneration is one of the many lies that the god of this world has used to blind the minds of unbelievers so they might not see the light of the gospel of the glory of Christ (2 Corinthians 4:4). He uses his false teachers and their religion to shut the kingdom of God from those trying to enter. Jesus said, "Woe to you, scribes and Pharisees, hypocrites, because you shut off the kingdom of heaven from men; for you do not enter in yourselves, nor do you allow those who are entering to go in" (Mat 23:13). False teachers point people to the broad gate. Jesus said, "Enter by the narrow gate; for the gate is wide, and the way is broad that leads to destruction, and many are those who enter by it. The gate is small, and the way is narrow that leads to life, and few are those who find it" (Matthew 7:13–14). One of the reasons only a few find the narrow gate is because very few believers are pointing people to "the way, the truth and the life" (John 14:6).

When we examine ourselves we need to examine the source and object of our faith. We must check which door we have gone through (*the narrow or the wide*), and which group we are in (*the few or the many*). It is easy to be deceived because both doors bear the same sign: "The Way to Heaven." One door is the Lord Jesus while the other is a counterfeit Jesus cleverly crafted by Satan. The narrow way that leads to life is paved with divine accomplishment while the wide road is built on man's achievements. One road has few travelers, the other has many who have been deceived and do not even know it. Those on the narrow road have strived to enter it. They have humbled themselves under the sovereign hand of God. They have mourned for their sins and hungered and thirsted for righteousness.

Those Catholics with spurious faith have believed the teachings of men and *think* they have been saved by the will of man, cleansed by the water of baptism, and sealed by the sacramental spirit of confirmation. Those who have true faith have believed the Word of God, been saved by the will of God, been cleansed by the blood of the Son of God, and sealed by the Spirit of God.

Part 3

An Eternity with Christ

19

No One Can Merit God's Grace

Satan's greatest lie may be that good works can help sinners escape the punishment of hell and merit the joy of heaven. This lie is used by all world religions to control people and hold them in legalistic bondage. It may be the most damning lie perpetrated on the human race because by it the saving grace of God is nullified by man's worthless works (Romans 11:6). Since grace, the unmerited favor of God, is the only means by which God saves sinners, anyone attempting to merit eternal life has instead earned death (Romans 6:23). Only by God's grace do we get what we don't deserve—heaven. And only by His mercy do we avoid getting what we do deserve–hell.

The only work that can save sinners is the work of Christ. Jesus Christ finished the work that was impossible for finite man to do (Psalm 49:7–8). He paid the eternal debt for sin and lived the perfect life required for entrance into heaven. Christ died "for sins once for all, the just for the unjust, in order that He might bring us to God" (1 Peter 3:18). By His death and resurrection He completed the work of man's redemption. Thus, for sinful man to believe his works can add to, co-mingle with, complement, or surpass the perfect work of Christ is an insult to God's holiness and justice.

Why then are we exhorted to be zealous for good works and to work out our salvation with fear and trembling   (Titus 2:14; Philippians 2:12)? And why does James say that man is justified by works and not by faith alone (James 2:24)? Let us search the Scriptures.

Three Elements of Salvation

First we must understand that there are three tenses in salvation. For believers in the Lord Jesus Christ salvation is past (justification), present (sanctification) and pending (glorification). This is why the Bible reveals that Christians have been saved, are being saved, and will be saved. All Christians have been saved (past tense) from the penalty of sin. Paul writes, "you have been saved through faith…not as a result of works" (Ephesians 2:8). At the moment of faith, the sinner is justified and has a right standing before God that is permanent (Hebrews 10:14). He cannot be condemned again (Romans 8:1). After justification believers begin working out (literally exercising) their salvation with fear and trembling (sanctification) by doing the good works God has prepared for them (Ephesians 2:10). Sanctification is an ongoing process whereby Jesus is manifested in Christians which saves them from the power of sin (2 Corinthians 4:11). Paul wrote: "To us who are being saved, it (the message of the cross) is the power of God" (1 Corinthians 1:18). Glorification is still future and will not occur until Jesus saves believers from the presence of sin. The Bible reveals: "Christ…will appear a second time, not to bear sin, but to bring salvation to those who are waiting for Him" (Hebrews 9:28).

Justification Is Not A Result of Works

Paul wrote: "The one who does not work, but believes in Him who justifies the ungodly, his faith is reckoned as righteousness" (Romans 4:5). In another passage we see "man is justified by faith apart from works of the Law" (Romans 3:28). Those who believe they can gain a right standing before God with their works and their own righteousness do not know God or His gospel (Romans 10:1–4). If they knew the righteousness of God they would know that all their righteous works are like filthy rags in His sight (Isaiah 64:6). They would know that the only way to approach Him would be with empty hands of faith, bringing nothing except their sins. As the hymnwriter Augustus Toplady wrote in his classic hymn "Rock of Ages," "nothing in my hands I bring, simply to Thy cross I cling." All human works prior to justifying faith are not acceptable to God because "without faith it is impossible to please Him" (Hebrews 11:6). The Bible clearly states over and over again that works are unable to secure salvation. "By the works of the Law no flesh will be justified" (Romans 3:20; Galatians 2:16). Salvation is "not on the basis of deeds which we have done in righteousness" (Titus 3:5). God saved us "not according to our works" (2 Timothy 1:9). Even works done in the name of Christ will not secure salvation (Matthew 7:22-23). Salvation is based entirely on God's doing so "that no man should boast before God" (1 Corinthians 1:29; Romans 4:2).

Reconciling James and Paul

James appears to contradict Paul when he writes: "You see that a man is justified by works, and not by faith alone" (James 2:24). Is one apostle contradicting another? No, it is because Paul is dealing with the nature of justification and James is dealing with the nature of faith. James is asking professing Christians, who have not shown any evidence for their new life in Christ, to "show me your faith" (James 2:18). But faith is invisible to man. It is an unseen relationship between man and God. Since faith cannot be seen, the best way to prove one's faith is to be "doers of the Word and not merely hearers" (James 1:22). Those who do the Word of God will live a righteous life in obedience to God. That is why James said: "I will show you my faith by my works" (James 2:18).

Faith alone justifies, but faith that justifies is never alone. As one great theologian, Dr. John H. Gerstner, was wont to say, "We are justified by faith alone, but not by a faith that is alone." True faith gives evidence of its existence by righteous living. James is concerned for professing Christians who have dead faith that is idle, barren, and unfruitful (James 2:17). He is saying that dead faith does not justify and is useless (James 2:20). Only genuine faith is alive and bears fruit. James is saying that a man who claims to have a right relationship with God will live a life of good works. You cannot have faith without works nor justification without sanctification.

Jesus said that by bearing fruit you "prove to be My disciples" (John 15:8). When there is no fruit it is a sign there is no relationship with the Savior. Jesus also taught that a tree is known by its fruit (Matthew 7:16–20). Just as works do not produce justification, the fruit does not bring the tree into existence. It only reveals the type of tree that it is.

Works Will Be Tested

Only some of the works done after justification are intrinsically good and acceptable to God. All the works of a Christian will be tested by fire. The good works, described by Paul as gold, silver, and precious stones, will survive the fire and result in rewards at the Bema seat. They are works done in faith, motivated by a love of God, in obedience to the will of God and for His glory. The worthless works are described as wood, hay, and straw. They will be burned up, and the believer shall suffer the loss of rewards (1 Corinthians 3:12–15).

Four Tests for Good Works

1. The timing of the works performed. They must be done after justification, not before (Ephesians 2:10; Philippians 2:12; 1 Thessalonians 1:3).

2. The motivation for the works. They must be done in love and thanksgiving for being chosen and redeemed by God, not to merit salvation (1 Corinthians 6:20; 1 Thessalonians 5:18).

3. The power through which the works are accomplished. They must be accomplished through faith in God's power, not through the power of man's flesh (John 15:5; Romans 15:13; Colossians 1:29; 2 Thessalonians 1:11; Hebrews 11:6).

4. The glory the works produce. They must glorify God, not man (Acts 4:21; Matthew 5:16; John 15:8; 1 Corinthians 10:31; Colossians 3:23; 1 Peter 2:12).

Worthless works will fail all or some of these tests. They include all works done before justification, as well as works done after justification that either seek to earn God's favor or man's applause. An example is the rebuke given by Jesus to the scribes and Pharisees: "They do all their deeds to be noticed by men; for they broaden their phylacteries, and lengthen the tassels of their garments" (Matthew 23:5). Paul wrote of those who "profess to know God, but by their deeds they deny Him, being detestable and disobedient, and worthless for any good deed" (Titus 1:16).

Roman Catholic Justification

Justification in the Roman Catholic Church is based on faith plus works to the extent that Catholics are condemned if they believe they are justified by faith alone. Canon 9 of the Council of Trent states: "If anyone says that the sinner is justified by faith alone, meaning that nothing else is required to cooperate in order to obtain the grace of justification…let him be anathema." The Catholic Church states that the grace of justification comes not through faith, but through the sacraments, beginning with baptism. The sacraments conform Catholics to the righteousness of God. Catholics are taught that they can then merit the graces needed to attain eternal life through the sacraments, good works, and obeying the law. Catholics are taught that they must establish and maintain their own righteousness to enter heaven rather than seek God's righteousness. From the *Catechism of the Catholic Church* we read (1992): "Justification is conferred in Baptism, the sacrament of faith. It conforms us to the righteousness of God, who makes us inwardly just by the power of his mercy." And in paragraph 2027 we read: "Moved by the Holy Spirit, we can merit for ourselves and for others all the graces needed to attain eternal life."

In conclusion we are justified by grace—the unmerited and undeserved gift of God (Romans 3:24). We receive this gift by believing on the Lord Jesus Christ (Romans 5:1). Our faith is justified by our works; works are the evidence that we have received the divine nature.

20

We Must Get the Gospel Right

When Catholics hear the gospel presentation for the first time, they will often say it is no different from what they already believe. After a closer look they may discover that the Jesus of the Catholic Church is not the Jesus of the Scriptures. *The New Catechism of the Catholic Church* teaches a different Jesus. (Paragraph numbers from the Catechism are in parenthesis.)

- He is unable to save completely (2027)

- He is unable to save forever (1861)

- He is unable to atone for all sin (1030, 1471)

- He returns physically to earth daily (1374-78)

- He dies again and again every day (1367)

- He did not finish the work of redemption (1405)

- He is not the only mediator (969, 494)

- He is not the only Way (841)

The best way to prepare for eternity is to know the true Jesus. From the Scriptures we know that the Lord Jesus Christ is able to save sinners completely and forever. He atones for all sin and His work of redemption is finished. He will return to the earth in glory, the very same way He left, and every eye will see Him. Since Jesus was raised from the dead He cannot die again. He has declared victory over death! Jesus is God's perfect man and man's perfect God and the only mediator between God and man. He is the only way to God and the only name under heaven by which man can be saved.

Establish Authority for Truth

In preparing for eternity the major issue that needs to be dealt with is authority. Resolve the question: "In what or in whom will you trust for your eternal destiny?" Each person ultimately must choose between man and his teachings or Jesus and His Word. To choose the latter is the safest and wisest decision anyone will ever make because Jesus is the truth (John 14:6). His word is truth (John 17:17) and He came to testify to the truth (John 18:37). Furthermore, every religious leader must be held accountable to Scriptural authority (Acts 17:11). No man or pope is infallible (Galatians 2:11–14) and tradition must never suppress the authority of God's Word (Mark 7:7–13; Colossians 2:8).

Understand Terms Biblically

We must understand the true meaning of essential terms of the gospel because the Vatican has redefined many of its key words. To Catholics "justification" is not God imputing the righteousness of Christ, but the process through which one conforms to righteousness; "sin" is not always mortal because lesser (venial) sins do not cause death; "repentance" is not a change of mind, but acts of penance or punishment Catholics must do to be absolved of their sin; "eternal life" is not eternal because spiritual life terminates whenever mortal sins are committed.

Understand the Bad News

What does God's justice demand as punishment for sin? The truth must be made known. God imposes the death penalty when His law is broken. The wages of sin is death (Romans 6:23). The second death is the eternal lake of fire where the unredeemed will pay the eternal punishment for sin (Revelation 20:14). People must first understand they are condemned before they will see their need for a Savior. They must know they are hopelessly lost before they seek God's provision. They must know that they are sick before they will ever seek a cure.

Understand and Believe the Gospel

It is easy to get lost in the complexity of the Catholic religion. Therefore, reject any tradition that leads you away from the saving power of the gospel (Romans 1:16). Jesus Christ is sufficient—His perfect and finished sacrifice (Hebrews 10:10–14), His grace (Romans 11:6), His Word (2 Timothy 3:15), His righteousness (1 Corinthians 1:30), and His intercession (Hebrews 7:25). The sufficiency of Christ is of utmost importance because Rome has added so many things that deny it. To His Word they add tradition; to His headship they add the pope; to His unique role as Mediator they add Mary; to His finished and complete sacrifice they add the Mass; to His high priestly office they add the confessional box; to His righteousness they add their own; to grace they add merit; to faith they add works; and to heaven and hell they add purgatory. It is only when Jesus is presented as the all-sufficient Savior that Catholics can be called to repent of these ungodly perversions of the gospel and be saved by Christ alone.

Receive What Jesus Offers

There are three promises Jesus offers to repentant sinners, which are totally foreign to most Catholics. They are (1) the complete forgiveness of sins; (2) the imputation of His perfect righteousness; and (3) the assurance of eternal life. These promises are foreign to Catholics because their church opposes them with a vengeance. The church councils (Trent and Vatican II) condemn any Catholic who believes these promises of God with an anathema. Rather than trust Jesus for the complete forgiveness of sins, Catholics look to purgatory and indulgences to pay for the residual sin and punishment that still remain. Rather than receive the perfect righteousness of Christ by faith, Catholics seek their own righteousness through good works and sacraments. And, finally, rather than believe God's promise of eternal life, Catholics are taught that they are committing the "sin of presumption" if they claim to know with certainty they have eternal life. Jesus offers Catholics spiritual blessings that have never been proclaimed from their church. Clearly, for Catholics to believe the Good News, they must repent of the false gospel of works. Only then will Jesus save them completely and forever, and only then can they stand before a Holy God in the perfect righteousness of His Son.

The Need for Repentance

Since grace is the only means by which God saves sinners, anyone who attempts to merit salvation actually nullifies God's grace (Romans 11:6). Catholics must therefore be persuaded to come to Jesus with empty hands of faith. One illustration that has been effective in doing this is to imagine a set of monkey bars suspended over hell. Catholics are hanging and swinging from different rungs labeled baptism, good works, sacraments, indulgences, and the Mass because they are taught that these things will keep them out of hell. Now picture Jesus suspended between them and hell saying, "I am the only one who can save you, but you must first let go of the things that cannot save you." For Catholics this is a giant step of faith because it goes against everything they have been taught. If they are still hanging on when they die, it will be too late. They must let go and believe that Jesus will save them before they perish. This is a picture of the very first command of Jesus when He said, "Repent and believe the gospel" (Mark 1:15).

Believe the Word of God

There is no match for the Word of God. It is living and powerful and sharper than any two-edged sword (Hebrews 4:12). Let it speak for itself. It is your only trustworthy authority for the most critical decision in life. We can be wrong about a lot of things in this life and still survive, but if we are wrong about the gospel when we die, we will pay for that mistake for all eternity. Everyone will be responsible to God for what He has revealed to us. The excuse, "I did everything my priest told me to do" will be a pitiful and wailing response after Jesus says, "Depart from me, I never knew you." While there is still time, respond to the exhortation of Paul, "Examine yourselves to see whether you are in the faith; test yourselves. Do you not realize that Christ Jesus is in you—unless, of course, you fail the test" (2 Corinthians 13:5)?

> *If you confess with your mouth Jesus as Lord and believe in your heart that God raised Him from the dead, you shall be saved, for with the heart man believes, resulting in righteousness, and with the mouth he confesses, resulting in salvation. Whoever will call upon the name of the Lord will be saved (Romans 10:9–10, 13).*

21

The Greatest Gift Ever Given

God's Perfection—He Is Holy

God is majestic in holiness (Exodus 15:11). Righteousness and justice are the foundation of His throne (Psalm 97:2). God is a righteous judge (Psalm 7:11). He cannot tolerate wickedness (Habakkuk 1:13). Nothing in all creation is hidden from God's sight. Everything is uncovered and laid bare before the eyes of Him to whom we must give an account (Hebrews 4:13). Those who worship God must worship in spirit and truth (John 4:24).

Man's Problem—All Have Sinned

There is no one righteous, not even one (Romans 3:10). All of us have become like one who is unclean, and all our righteous acts are like filthy rags (Isaiah 64:6). All have sinned and fall short of the glory of God (Romans 3:23). Your iniquities have separated you from your God; and your sins have hidden His face from you (Isaiah 59:2).

The wrath of God is revealed from heaven against all ungodliness (Romans 1:18). The soul who sins shall die (Ezekiel 18:4). The lake of fire is the second death (Revelation 20:14). Unless a man is born again, he cannot see the king God's Provision—A Savior.

Jesus Christ is the blessed hope...our great God and Savior (Titus 2:13). He is the image of the invisible God...in Him all the fullness of Deity dwells in bodily form (Colossians. 1:15; 2:9). For God so loved the world, that He gave His only begotten Son, that whoever believes in Him should not perish, but have eternal life (John 3:16). God made Him (Jesus) who knew no sin to be sin on our behalf, that we might become the righteousness of God in Him (2 Corinthians 5:21).

Christ was sacrificed once to take away the sins of many people (Hebrews 9:28). Christ suffered once for sins, the just for the unjust, that He might bring us to God (1 Peter 3:18). He (Jesus) is able to save completely those who come to God through Him (Hebrews 7:25). There is salvation in no one else, for there is no other name under heaven given among men by which we must be saved (Acts 4:12).

Man's Part—Repent and Believe

Repent and believe the gospel (Mark 1:15). Godly sorrow brings repentance that leads to salvation (2 Corinthians 7:10). The gospel is the power of God for the salvation of all who believe it (Romans 1:16). By this gospel you are saved...that Christ died for our sins...that He was buried, that He was raised on the third day according to the Scriptures (1 Corinthians 15:2-4).

If you confess with your mouth, "Jesus is Lord," and believe in your heart that God raised Him from the dead, you will be saved. For it is with your heart that you believe and are justified and with your mouth that you confess and are saved (Romans 10:9-10). Believe in the Lord Jesus Christ and you will be saved (Acts 16:31).

God's Promise—Eternal Life

God has given us eternal life, and this life is in His Son. He who has the Son has the life; he who does not have the Son of God does not have the life. These things I have written to you who believe in the name of the Son of God, in order that you may know that you have eternal life (1 John 5:11-13).

Whoever believes in the Son has eternal life, but whoever rejects the Son will not see life for God's wrath remains on Him (John 3:36). I give them eternal life, and they shall never perish; no one can snatch them out of my hand. My Father who has given them to me is greater than all; no one can snatch them out of my Father's hand (John 10:28–29). God's gifts and His call are irrevocable (Rom. 11:29).

Man's Privilege—Serve The King

Yet to all who received Him, to those who believed in His name, He gave the right to become children of God, ambassadors for Christ and citizens of heaven (John 1:12; Phil. 3:20; 2 Cor. 5:19-20). Go into all the world and preach the good news to all creation (Mark 16:15).

How Will You Respond to God's Word?

Jesus said He will judge those who reject Him and His Word (John 12:48). He also said if you do not believe He is who He claims to be, you will die in your sins (John 8:24). There is only one way to be saved—by grace alone, through faith alone, in Christ alone. "For by grace you have been saved through faith, and that not of yourselves; it is the gift of God, not of works, lest anyone should boast." (Ephesians 2:8-9). And if by grace, then it is no longer by works; if it were, grace would no longer be grace (Romans 11:6). You must cease from trusting in anything you DO to save yourself and put all your trust in Jesus and what He has DONE—His sacrificial death on Calvary's cross and His resurrection from the dead. This will give you a permanent right standing before God!

How will you escape if you neglect so great a salvation? Now is the day of salvation (2 Corinthians 6:2).dom of God (John 3:3).

22

Hard Questions for Good Catholics

Two thousand years ago the Lord Jesus had some hard questions for good Jews. He asked questions not only to make His gospel known, but also to expose the errors of religious leaders. Most of His questions need to be asked of religious leaders today.

Jesus challenged Nicodemus, a ruler of the Jews, about his knowledge of the Kingdom of God: "Are you the teacher of Israel and do not understand these things?" (John 3:10). He asked the stubborn-hearted Pharisees who were blinded by religious tradition: "If I speak the truth, why do you not believe Me?" (John 8:46). Then He exposed how corrupt their religion had become with this hard question: "Why do you break the command of God for the sake of your tradition?" (Matthew 15:3). Possibly the most important question the Son of God ever asked was addressed to Peter: "Who do you say that I am?" (Matthew 16:15). The response to this question carries eternal consequences because Jesus warned: "If you do not believe that I am [the one I claim to be], you will indeed die in your sins" (John 8:24). These questions must be answered correctly not only by those lost in religion, but by everyone else. Here are some hard questions to ask good Catholics.

Where do you go to find the truth about life's most critical issues?

There is only one source that will never mislead you, never deceive you, or try to control you. It is Christ and His Word (John 14:6; 17:17). Jesus said: "If you abide in My word…you shall know the truth, and the truth shall make you free" (John 8:31–32). Free from what? Free from many things, but certainly the bondage of religious deception. Knowledge of the truth is necessary to escape from the snare of the devil who holds people captive to do his will (2 Timothy 2:25–26). Satan uses deceitful workers who disguise themselves as apostles of Christ to blind people from the truth (2 Corinthians 11:13–15). In spite of this, Rome defiantly declares its bishops to be successors of the "apostles of Christ." According to the *Catechism of the Catholic Church* (CCC), "Whoever listens to them is listening to Christ" (CCC, para. 862). The apostles had only two successors—Matthias, who was chosen by the apostles, and Paul, who was chosen by Christ (Acts 9:1–19). Catholic bishops do not meet the qualifications for apostleship given in Acts 1:21–26.

God warns us: "Do not trust in princes, in mortal man, in whom there is no salvation" (Psalm 146:3). Why the warning? Because "savage wolves will come in among you, not sparing the flock; and from among your own selves men will arise, speaking perverse things, to draw away the disciples after them" (Acts 20:29–30). In light of these warnings, a most critical question must be answered truthfully: Do you trust Christ and His Word or man and his religious traditions?

Did you know there is only one way to be saved?

God's gospel is the message of salvation by grace through faith in one person (Ephesians 2:8–9). The gift of eternal life is given freely to those who trust the eternal God incarnate–Jesus Christ–His virgin birth, His perfect life, His atoning death, and His glorious resurrection (1 Corinthians 15:1–4). The Lord Jesus is sufficient to save sinners completely and forever. Diametrically opposed to God's gospel is the Catholic gospel that offers salvation through baptism. Newborn babes who receive the sacrament of baptism are said to be saved apart from personal faith in Jesus. The Catholic priest believes he is replacing the sovereign work of God by administering baptism. The sacrament "not only purifies all sins, but also makes the neophyte a new creature, an adopted son of God who has become a partaker of the divine nature, a member of Christ and co-heir with Him, and a temple of the Holy Spirit" (CCC, 1257, 1265).

Did you know those who distort the gospel are condemned?

This includes apostles, priests, popes, pastors, or angels (apparitions of Mary) from heaven. The Apostle Paul warned: "There are some who…want to distort the gospel of Christ. But even though we, or an angel from heaven, should preach to you a gospel contrary to that which we have preached to you, let him be accursed" (Galatians 1:7–8). Catholics need to be warned that their clergy is under divine condemnation for adding works and sacraments to God's gospel (CCC, 1129).

Did you know that Jesus put an end to the ordained priesthood?

God's Word reveals that the veil of the temple that separated the Holy of Holies from sinful man was torn open by God (Matthew 27:51). Man can now come directly to God through faith in the shed blood of the Savior (Romans 3:23–26). Priests are no longer needed to offer sacrifices for sin (Hebrews 10:18). The only legitimate priesthood that remains on earth is the royal priesthood of all believers. They offer sacrifices of praise and thanksgiving for being called out of darkness into the marvelous light of the Son (1 Peter 2:9).

Do you really believe Catholic priests have the power to call the Lord Jesus down from heaven every day?

According to Roman Catholic priest John O'Brien in his book *Faith of Millions*: "The priest…reaches up into the heavens, brings Christ down from His throne, and places Him upon our altar to be offered up again as the Victim for the sins of man…Christ, the eternal and omnipotent God, bows his head in humble obedience to the priest's command." Over 200,000 times each day, priests throughout the world believe they represent Jesus on their altars as an offering for sins of the living and the dead (CCC, 1371-1374). Again Catholics ignore God's Word that declares that Jesus "having been offered once to bear the sins of many, *shall appear a second time* for salvation *not to bear sin*" (Hebrews 9:28). The Bible also tells us *how* and *when* Jesus will appear. He will return the same way he left, with power and great glory (Matthew 24:27–30; Acts 1:11). By the authority of God's Word we must conclude that the Eucharist presents a false Christ who is deceiving millions.

Why do Catholic priests continue to offer Jesus as a sacrificial victim when He said "It is finished" (John 19:30)?

God's Word says that Jesus appeared *once* and offered Himself *once* to bear sins. His offering is not to be done again (Hebrews 9:25–28). When Jesus "offered *one* sacrifice for sins for all time, (He) sat down at the right hand of God" (Hebrews 10:12). Disregarding the infallible Word of God, Catholicism teaches: "The sacrifice of Christ and the sacrifice of the Eucharist are one single sacrifice. The victim is one and the same. In this divine sacrifice, the same Christ who offered himself once…is contained and offered in an unbloody manner" (1367).

Did you know that Jesus has already obtained redemption for believers?

Catholicism denies this by teaching: "The work of our redemption is carried on" every time the Eucharist is celebrated (CCC, 1405). God's Word declares: "He [Jesus] entered the holy place once for all, having obtained eternal redemption" (Hebrews 9:12). "In Him we have redemption through His blood, the forgiveness of our trespasses, according to the riches of His grace" (Ephesians 1:7).

Why do you call Jesus the Savior when you must save yourself?

Catholicism teaches the sinner must "make satisfaction for" or "expiate" his sins. This satisfaction is also called "penance" (1459). "In this way they attained their own salvation and co-operated in saving their brothers" (1477). God's Word proclaims: "There is salvation in no one else; for there is no other name under heaven given among men, by which we must be saved" (Acts 4:12).

Why do you believe a place called Purgatory can purify your sins?

God's Word says" "When He [Jesus] had made purification of sins, He sat down at the right hand of the Majesty on high" (Hebrews 1:3). "He gave Himself for us to...purify for Himself a people for His own possession" (Titus 2:14). "The blood of Jesus...cleanses us from all sin" (1 John 1:7). These verses destroy the myth of Purgatory. Yet the Vatican continues to deceive Catholics by teaching that they "must undergo purification [in Purgatory] to achieve the holiness necessary to enter the joy of heaven" (CCC, 1030).

Why do you pray to Mary?

Nowhere in the Bible do we see believers praying to anyone except God. Jesus taught us how to pray in the Sermon on the Mount. He instructed us to pray to the Father and not to use meaningless repetition (Matthew 6:7–13). Yet Catholics are taught to pray the rosary, that is made up of over 50 meaningless and repetitious prayers to Mary.

Why aren't these Catholic traditions found in the 1st century Church?

- Priests offering sacrifices for sins

- Indulgences to remit sin's punishment

- Prayers for those in purgatory

- Church leaders forbidden to marry

- Infallible men

- Salvation dispensed through sacrament

Did you know that whenever you believe a doctrine, you must also forsake that which opposes it?

Scripture reveals that Jesus saves:

- by faith in Him, not baptism

- by His grace, not our merit

- by His finished work, not our works

- by His righteousness, not ours

- by His one offering for sin, not the Mass

- by His blood, not purgatory

- by His obedience, not ours

- by His gospel, not a perversion of it

Which Jesus will you trust?

The Jesus of the Bible promises eternal life, the complete forgiveness of sins, a permanent right standing with God, and the power to live a victorious life. The Catholic Jesus is a Jesus that was never preached by the apostles (2 Corinthians 11:4). This counterfeit Christ provides only conditional life, partial forgiveness of sins, and an ongoing need for priests and mediators. The Catholic Jesus offers only uncertainty, fear, and doubt. Those who reject the true Jesus, who is revealed in His *Word*, will be judged accordingly. The Lord Jesus Christ said, "The word I spoke is what will judge him at the last day" (John 12:48).

Part 4

Equipping The Saints

23

Are You Prepared to Meet the Lord Jesus?

Jesus said, "Not everyone who says to Me, 'Lord, Lord,' will enter the kingdom of heaven; but he who does the will of My Father" (Matthew 7:21). There have always been people who called Jesus "Lord," but did not do what He says (Luke 6:46). Tragically there are many professing Christians who will face Him on Judgment Day and hear these terrifying words: "I never knew you; depart from Me, you who practice lawlessness" (Matthew 7:22). Churches are filled with victims of "another gospel." Others have been misled by man-centered methods of evangelism.

When we consider the sobering words of the Lord Jesus, it would be wise for us to examine ourselves to make sure we are in the faith (2 Corinthians 13:5). A thoughtful examination of our faith will prepare us to meet the Lord Jesus Christ. Following are nine exhortations the Bible gives to insure our faith conforms to the faith of the apostles.

Believe Jesus as the Truth

How do you know whom to believe? There are many who speak for God; however, you must believe in Him whom God has sent (John 6:29). God the Father sent His Son Jesus to bear witness to the truth. Jesus is the personification of truth and His word is truth (John 14:6; 17:17). There is therefore no higher authority than Christ and His Word. There is no one who is more trustworthy! Everyone who is of the truth will hear His voice (John 18:37). Do not dishonor Jesus by taking someone else's word over His. Do not be deceived! Test everything with the Word of God. The Bible is what God says; religion is what *man says* God says.

Fear Jesus as Your Judge

The fear of the Lord is the beginning of wisdom (Proverbs 1:7). It is appointed for men to die once and after this comes judgment (Hebrews 9:27). He who rejects Jesus and does not receive His sayings, those words will judge him at the last day (John 12:48). He who hears His Word and believes Him has eternal life and does not come into judgment (John 5:24). If we go on sinning willfully after receiving the knowledge of the truth, we can expect a certain terrifying judgment and a consuming fire (Hebrews 10:27).

Receive Jesus as Your New Life

To those who received Him by believing in His name, He gave the right to become children of God, born not of blood, nor of the will of the flesh, nor of the will of man, but of God (John 1:12–13). He who has Jesus has the life; he who does not have the Son of God does not have the life (1 John 5:12). They remain dead in sin (Ephesians 2:5).

Trust Jesus as the Lamb of God

Behold, the Lamb of God who takes away the sin of the world (John 1:29). All of us have sinned and are guilty before God. His holiness and justice demand that all sin be punished by death (Romans 3:23; 6:23). But as the perfect sacrificial Lamb, Christ died for sins once for all, the righteous for the unrighteous (1 Peter 3:18). The death of Jesus satisfied the demands of God's justice, thereby enabling Him to forgive and save those who trust Him (Romans 3:26). God forgives all their transgressions, and no punishment or purging remains (Colossians 2:13–14). Only by God's grace and mercy can sinners be saved (Ephesians 2:8, 9; Titus 3:5). You must cease from trusting anyone or anything else (2 Corinthians 3:5).

Obey Jesus as the Son of God

Jesus became the source of eternal salvation to all who obey Him (Hebrews 5:8). We know we have come to know Him if we keep His commandments (1 John 2:3). His first command is "Repent and believe the gospel" (Mark 1:14). "Repent" means to change your mind when confronted with the truth about God, sin, judgment, and salvation. Repentance is characterized by turning from sin and idols to God (1 Thessalonians 1:9). God declares all men must repent, and unless you repent you will perish (Acts. 17:30; Luke 13:3). Godly sorrow brings repentance that leads to salvation (2 Corinthians 7:10). To "believe the gospel" means to trust Jesus and His Word. He who believes in the Son has eternal life; but he who does not obey the Son shall not see life, but the wrath of God abides on him (John 3:36). Those who do not know God and do not obey the gospel of our Lord Jesus will pay the penalty of eternal destruction (2 Thessalonians 1:8–9).

Follow Jesus as the Only Way

Jesus said, "I am the way…no one comes to the Father but through Me" (John 14:6). Since He is the only one who came from heaven and returned, we must follow Him (John 3:13). Jesus said, "If anyone wishes to come after Me, let him deny himself, and take up his cross daily, and follow Me" (Luke 9:23). There is only one narrow way that leads to life, but there is a [another] way that seems right to a man, but its end is the way of death (Proverbs 14:12).

Come to Jesus as the Only Mediator

There is one God and one mediator between God and men, the man Christ Jesus (1 Timothy 2:5). He is God's perfect man and man's perfect God, and the only One who can change a sinner's relationship with God from one of hostility to one of peace. Do not attempt to approach God through any other mediator because no one else is qualified. Pray only to God in the name of His Son.

Confess Jesus as Lord

If you confess with your mouth Jesus as Lord, and believe in your heart that God raised Him from the dead, you shall be saved; for with the heart man believes, resulting in righteousness, and with the mouth he confesses, resulting in salvation (Romans 10:9–10).

Embrace Jesus as Your Righteousness

The gift of Christ's righteousness is given only to those who repent and believe the gospel (Romans 5:17; 1 Corinthians 1:30; Hebrews 10:14). This righteousness, which comes from God, is on the basis of faith—though not as a reward for it (Philippians 3:9). There is no other way to have a right standing before God. The righteous deeds of an unbeliever are like a filthy garment and must be forsaken (Isaiah 64:6).

If you have repented and believed the gospel then you have received eternal life as a gift of God's grace. Lest you ever forget, God has saved you for a purpose—to glorify Him in word and deed! Following are some exhortations for those who have been born of God.

Proclaim Jesus as the Only Savior

Proclaim the excellencies of Him who has called you out of darkness into His marvelous light (1 Peter 2:9). There is salvation in no one else; for there is no other name under heaven that has been given among men by which we must be saved (Acts 4:12). Jesus is the only one who can forgive us and deliver us from the power and penalty of sin.

Love Jesus as Sovereign God

Love the Lord your God with all your heart, soul, and mind (Matthew 22:37). Demonstrate your love by walking according to His commandments (2 John 1:6).

Praise Jesus as Your Advocate

Let everyone who names the Lord Jesus abstain from wickedness; but if you do sin, you have an Advocate with the Father (2 Timothy 2:19; 1 John 2:1).

Glorify Jesus as Your Redeemer

You have been bought with a price; therefore glorify God in your body (1 Corinthians 6:20). In Him we have redemption through His blood, the forgiveness of our trespasses, according to the riches of His grace (Ephesians 1:7).

Worship Jesus as Holy God

Holy, holy, holy, is the Lord God, the Almighty, who was and who is and who is to come (Revelation 4:8). Present your bodies a living and holy sacrifice, acceptable to God, which is your spiritual service of worship (Romans 12:1). Do not worship Jesus in vain by following the traditions of men (Mark 7:7). Do not become futile in your speculations by exchanging the glory of the incorruptible God for an image (Romans 1:23).

Look to Jesus as your only Priest

As a merciful and faithful high priest, He satisfied divine justice by offering Himself once for all sin for all time (Hebrews 2:17; 10:12). At that moment God tore open the veil to the holy of holies (Matthew 27:51). Repentant sinners now have access to the Father through faith in His shed blood (Ephesians 2:18). Since there are no more offerings for sin, do not dishonor Jesus by participating in ongoing offerings by other priests (Hebrews 10:18). By His one offering, He has perfected for all time those who are sanctified (Hebrews 10:14).

Serve Jesus as Your Master

No one can serve two masters. Either he will hate the one and love the other, or he will hold to one and despise the other. You cannot serve God and mammon (Matthew 6:24). Since we receive a kingdom that cannot be shaken, let us show gratitude by offering to God an acceptable service with reverence and awe (Hebrews 12:28). Jesus said, "If anyone serves Me, let him follow Me; and where I am, there shall My servant also be; if anyone serves Me, the Father will honor him" (John 12:26).

Long for Jesus as your Blessed Hope

Look for the blessed hope and the appearing of the glory of our great God and Savior, Christ Jesus (Titus 2:13). What a glorious day that will be for all who have responded with faith and obedience to the Lord Jesus!

Until that glorious day, we know that those who are faithful to Christ and His Word will suffer persecution, ridicule, insults, and ostracism. May we all be comforted by the words of Peter: "If anyone suffers as a Christian, let him not feel ashamed, but in that name let him glorify God. For it is time for judgment to begin with the household of God; and if it begins with us first, what will be the outcome for those who do not obey the gospel of God? And, if it is with difficulty that the righteous is saved, what will become of the godless man and the sinner? Therefore, let those also who suffer according to the will of God entrust their souls to a faithful Creator in doing what is right" (1 Peter 4:16–19).

24

Answers to Questions from Catholics

Over the years we have answered hundreds of questions from Roman Catholics using the power and confidence of God's Word. Some of them have been little more than vitriolic attacks on me, and some of them have been earnest inquiries for truth. As a means to equip you with biblical answers to similar questions, we have provided a sampling of their letters and emails along with my responses.

Crisis of Faith

I am 44 years old and have been a Catholic for 13 years. My faith journey has brought me to this crossroad where I question a lot of the Catholic Dogma and wonder if these are the "rituals" I want to practice. I hesitate leaving the Church, especially with a child I've coerced through 1st Communion. How would I explain it to her? I've also been teaching CCD [Confraternity of Christian Doctrine] and RCIA [Rite of Christian Initiation for Adults] and I am a Eucharistic Minister. I've resigned all those duties within the last few months due to the status of my faith journey. D.E., Fresno, CA

Response

God seeks worshippers in Spirit and Truth (John 4:24). If the church you are worshipping in does not teach the pure truth of God's word, you must honor God by finding one that does.

The best way to explain to your daughter why you are leaving is with the authority of the Bible. Explain to her that you have been deceived because you followed the teachings and traditions of men rather than the Word of God. Tell her that you now want to honor God by finding a church where you can worship Him in truth and grow in the grace of knowledge of our Lord Jesus Christ.

Truth Mixed with Error

I was surfing the internet and came across your web site and your ministry to Catholics. I have come to Jesus "by faith alone through Scripture alone." There are a few things in Catholicism that I think are correct and that is what keeps me going to the Catholic Church. What bothers me is that Rome insists that we Catholics must believe everything. Are they so unsure of their position that they must have 100% thought control? I really don't know the reason. T.S., Landing, NJ

Response

Indeed, there are a few things in the Catechism that are correct. However, you have discovered something that many Catholics refuse to acknowledge. The Catholic religious system holds its people in bondage by covering its deceptive teachings with a veneer of truth. Catholics are taught that salvation is dispensed through the sacraments. Attendance at Mass and membership in the church is necessary under the threat of eternal condemnation. These are lies that blind Catholics from the truth of the gospel. Jesus said, " If you abide in My Word, then you are truly disciples of Mine, and you shall know the truth, and the truth shall make you free" (John 8:31–32). Let the chains fall off that hold you captive in the bondage of deception. Find a church that teaches the truth, the whole truth, and nothing but the truth.

The Bible was Forbidden

In one of your publications you stated that in the 16th century a Catholic priest would refuse to absolve a person's sin in the confessional box if they had possession of a Bible. Please tell me where you came up with this non-truth? Don, Internet

Response

It is found in the *Canons and Degrees of the Council of Trent* by Reverend Schroeder with Nihil Obstate ["Nothing Offensive"] and Imprimatur under the section, "Ten Rules Concerning Prohibited Books by Pope Pius." Rule #4 reads: "Those who presume to read or possess the Sacred Books of the Bible without permission may not receive absolution from their sins till they have handed them over to the ordinary."

The Eucharist

I just read your article on the Eucharist and I am afraid you are very mistaken. Dr. Scott Hahn can help you on this topic and clear up the confusion. You are dividing and confusing Christians, especially Catholics who love and adore Jesus and His Church. St. Paul was very passionate in his letters about disciples causing disunity among believers. Are you aware of the miracles associated with the Eucharist and the love of the Blessed Virgin Mary in her Seven Sorrows. You are just one man claiming to know more than a Magisterium, the fathers of the church, and 2000 years of theological study by the most intelligent human beings on the planet. You have put yourself above Thomas Aquinas, Augustine, and the like. I hope you will discern with the guidance of the Holy Spirit the purpose, intent and affect of your anti-Catholic rhetoric. To cause such confusion seems to me as a misguided, fruitless mission. You are not doing anyone any favors by signaling out Catholics. In fact, you need to repent of this misguided pride and false pretense. The Catholic Church is the final authority on biblical interpretation. The theological genius and supernatural revelations given them are way beyond anything Protestants can touch. I'm not one of your victims of theological ignorance. Nor am I a weak uninformed Catholic Christian. Your attempt to "save" Catholics by discrediting the real presence of Christ in the Eucharist reveals the height of your error and pride. If you are suggesting I am a false convert by sending me your article, then your pride is deeper than I originally considered. Thousands of "Evangelical" people like you waste so much time using anti-catholic rhetoric to steam their cause. Can you imagine how the demons are laughing? Thank God for the Catholic Church. We have our heads screwed on straight while putting our spiritual energies towards countless good deeds. Elizabeth, Internet

Response

Your unbending loyalty to a religion is very similar to the fierce loyalty of the first century Jews. Many of them were so blinded by their corrupt religion that they did not recognize their promised Messiah. Just as the Jewish leaders nullified the Word of God with their traditions, the Catholic Church has done the same (Mark 7:6–13). You put yourself in the same peril as the Jews by trusting the teachings of men above the Word of God. In my article on the Eucharist I used the very words of Jesus to prove that He is not physically present. How appalling is it to teach that the glorified, risen Savior can be reduced to the inner substance of a wafer and then be eaten. You do not see the truth because a veil of blindness covers your heart. It will remain until you turn from your bishops and seek the truth in Christ and His Word (2 Corinthians 3:14–16). You accuse me of being prideful, but as you read my articles you can see that my boasting is only in the Lord Jesus and what He has done and is doing. It is clear from your letter that your religious pride has blinded you from the glory of Christ and His gospel (2 Corinthians 4:4). I sent you the article on "False Converts in the Church" because of my love for the many Protestants and Catholics who think they are on the way to heaven, but have never examined their faith to see if it is biblical. I pray you will do that now. Please know that doctrine is what divides believers from unbelievers. Jesus and Paul called for unity in the truth!

Apostolic Succession

I watched your YouTube series on "Catholicism vs. Evangelical Christianity." You are very well spoken, yet I feel if you really want to convince Catholics your way is the right way you'll need to go against a renowned Catholic Apologist like Dr. Scott Hahn. You do that debate and perhaps more heads will turn. As a Maronite Catholic I can't bring myself to go evangelical. You gave an impassioned plea, but I still believe Apostolic Succession means something. Having a Doctorate of Theology doesn't guarantee anything except that you're well educated. It's the laying on of hands that enables the priest to use the claim of apostolic succession and sacred tradition. Good luck in spreading the Word of God. To me, there is a difference between having some of the faith and the fullness of the faith. A Maronite Catholic, Greg, Internet

Response

It is not my objective to "convince" Catholics that "my way" is the right way. Our ministry is to point Roman Catholics and everyone else to the Word of God, which is the supreme authority for all matters of faith. Scripture is sufficient to make one wise unto salvation (2 Timothy 3:15–16). God has revealed the only way sinners can be forgiven of their sins and saved from eternal punishment. The Holy Spirit is the only one who can convince or convict those who are deceived (John 16:8–11). He does this by removing their spiritual blindness as they turn to Christ and His Word for truth (2 Corinthians 3:16). If you continue to look to your clergy or Scott Hahn for the truth, the spiritual blindness will remain. Scott Hahn became an apostate when he left a small Presbyterian Church to follow the deceitful spirits of the Catholic religion (1 Timothy 4:1). According to his testimony, he began praying the rosary and Mary answered his prayers. You may not know that praying to the dead is an ungodly practice that is an abomination to God (Deuteronomy 18:10–12). No God-fearing person in the Bible prayed to anyone except God. Perhaps you will now seek the truth from the only trustworthy source—Christ and His Word (John 14:6, 17:17).

Brennan Manning

"Proclaiming The Gospel" has been a blessing to me. Over the years, I have given your book, *Preparing Catholics For Eternity*, and your gospel tracts to Catholics. Some repented and turned to Christ alone, but one young priest became very angry with me. Lately, I have been talking to several pastors concerning their admiration of Brennan Manning. I shared some of your statements from the DVD, "God and the Gushy Gospel," such as, "Manning teaches a gospel that is full of mysticism, but void of the truth." Also, "He preaches a gospel of works and sacraments. He is an enemy of the gospel of Jesus Christ." The pastors took issue with me and defended Manning. Can you help me by clarifying his errors? I pastored a church for 50+ years, but these pastors tell me, "You are not relevant with this generation." I.H., Council Bluffs, IA

Response

Manning is an inactive Catholic priest who left the priesthood to get married, but now has divorced his wife. As a recovering alcoholic, he is heavy into contemplative prayer and Eastern mysticism. His popularity as a writer and speaker in evangelical circles continues to grow despite his proclamation of "another" gospel. Manning's gospel declares that all people are redeemed. In his book, *The Signature of Jesus*, he "looks upon human nature as fallen but redeemed, flawed but in essence good" (p. 125). He promotes a contemplative wordless "prayer" that involves breathing exercises and the chanting of a sacred word or phrase. He says, "the first step in faith is to stop thinking about God at the time of prayer" (p. 212). Man-ning dedicates an entire chapter to "Celebrate the Darkness." He must be unaware that God calls His people out of darkness and they should have nothing to do with it (2 Corinthians 6:14; Ephesians 5:8; 1 Thessalonians 5:4–5; 1 Peter 2:9; 1 John 1:5–10). His flawed theology and fatal gospel have a lot to do with his low view of Scripture. He writes: "I am deeply distressed by... the idolatry of the Scriptures. For many Christians, the Bible is not a pointer to God but God himself, in a word—bibliolatry" (pp. 188–89). Manning must not know that "the Word was God, became flesh and dwelt among us" (John 1:1, 14). These are just a few of the major problems with Brennan Manning. You are to be commended for warning others of his deceptive teachings.

Unbelieving Spouse

I have written and spoken with you before and each time I have received wonderful encouragement. I thank you for that and appreciate your ministry. My husband converted to Catholicism 10 years ago and he is now a teacher in the RCIA classes. I am a Bible-believing Christian and strongly disagree with my husband's conversion. After being married for 27 years, he has asked me to renew our wedding vows in the Catholic Church. As you can imagine this has caused much strife in our marriage. I want to honor my husband, but do not feel obligated to renew vows in a church that I strongly oppose. What do you think? Name withheld for privacy.

Response

You have a delicate situation, but I think it is clear from Scripture how you need to respond. You are to submit to your husband as he submits to Christ. Since he is asking you to do something against the Word of God you can decline. If we compromise God's standard for righteousness we weaken our witness and character. Christianity is incompatible with any form of a false religion. Paul makes this clear in 2 Corinthians 6:14–18: "What agreement has the temple of God with idols." In other words, it would not be wise to renew vows before God in a church filled with idols. We know throughout Scripture how God hates every false way. I would approach your husband with gentleness and humility and confirm your love and devotion to him. Explain to him that your love and devotion for Jesus will not allow you to participate in a ceremony performed by religious people who send people to hell with a false gospel. Ask him if there is another way you can renew your wedding vows in a way that honors him and your Savior. Please let me know his response.

Third Secret of Fatima

Can you refer me to info regarding the prophecies from *The Third Secret of Fatima?* I am witnessing to my brother, who claims to have an "in" on this info. I need to help lead him back to Truth. L.B., Internet

Response

I would encourage you to avoid getting sidetracked on rabbit trails that take you away from Christ and Him crucified (1 Corinthians 2:2). Those who have tested the spirits have found the Fatima apparitions to be ungodly and demonic (1 John 4:1). They bring demonic messages of deception that are opposed to God's Word (2 Corinthians 11:14; 1 Peter 5:8). The best way to lead him back to the truth is to establish Christ and His Word as the only infallible source for finding it (John 14:6; 17:17). Talking to him about demonic apparitions may lead him further into spiritual deception.

Catholic Baptist

What a great ministry you have to Catholics who are so very hard and in great bondage. I am now mentoring a lady I will call a Catholic/Baptist. I know that's an oxymoron, but she is clearly confused. She was brought up as a Baptist and then married a Catholic. She is stuck on several things. Jesus told His disciples that "If you forgive the sins of any, their sins have been forgiven them; if you retain the sins of any, they have been retained" (John 20:23). She said this is why Catholic priests are able to forgive sins. Whenever I bring up something she doesn't agree with she says, "That's YOUR interpretation, and that's why there are so many denominations." When Jesus said, "Upon this rock I will build my church," what is the rock? I'm praying that her eyes will be opened. M.M., Kernersville, NC

Response

If there is one verse on which the Roman Catholic religion stands or falls, it is Matthew 16:18. Rome says the rock upon which Jesus will build His church is Peter, however there is a more cogent interpretation. The rock is not Peter, but the content of his confession: "You are the Christ, the Son of the living God." Peter declared, from divine revelation, that Jesus is the Messiah/Christ. He is the only foundation that is immovable, indestructible, and infallible. Regarding your question on the forgiveness of sins, tell your friend that everyone born of the Spirit of God has the power to tell people their sins are forgiven, but only after they have repented and believed the gospel. The power is in the gospel (Romans 1:16). In the 37 years I confessed to a priest, not once did he present the gospel or ask me if I believed it. (See our website for more information on "the rock.")

Interpreting Scripture

I have watched a number of your interviews and read your materials. I'm profoundly saddened by your assumptions and misunderstanding of the Catholic faith. It isn't even close to reality. Why do you not read the Bread of Life (John 6) discourse literally? You seem to pick your scripture verses selectively. George, Internet

Response

Jesus told the woman drawing water at the well that He could give her living water and she would never thirst again (John 4:10). In John 6, He tells those who were following Him for more bread and another free lunch that He is the living bread and those who believe in Him shall never thirst (6:35). Anyone should be able to see Jesus was not speaking literally about never thirsting. He said His words were spirit (6:63). They are for spiritual nourishment. Jesus was using the everyday activity of "eating" to communicate how spiritual truths must be received. It is indeed an interesting analogy. Just as food is useless unless eaten, truth does no good unless it is internalized, believed, and acted upon. Just as no one eats if they are satisfied and full, no one will receive the truth of God's Word if they are satisfied with worldliness or full of religious traditions. Just as no one can eat for someone else, no one can receive and believe the gospel truth for anyone else. Faith is a personal matter and each sinner must repent and believe the gospel for salvation. I pray that you will take this literally. The sixth chapter of John is all about exchanging religion for an intimate relationship with Jesus Christ.

Gospel Tracts

I find it to be a shame that your ministry can't sell your version of "Christianity" without being deceitful about the Catholic Church. I support the woman from Pensacola who was angered about your promotion of lies in your pamphlet "Roman Catholicism, Scripture vs. Tradition." After John Martignoni exposed your clever-yet-bogus teachings about the Catholic Church, I had hope that you would be humble enough to retract your false claims against the Catholic Church. My hopes were unfulfilled. I can see that you are still selling your lies for $7 a pop. I guess truth is bad for your business. You said, "God chose 40 fallible men to pen His inspired, infallible Word, which should be everyone's supreme authority in matters of faith." Like a good salesman, part of this is true, but most of it is your fallible opinion, craftily stated, so it looks true. Where does the Bible claim to be "the supreme authority in matters of faith?" You said, "The Catholic religion sells indulgences as a means to gain God's favor," but where does the Church teach this? Where is this documented as an official teaching of the

Church? If you were an honest salesman, you would admit that the Church doesn't teach this. You said, "There are no competitors to His truth, only adversaries that twist and distort it." You might start by looking into the mirror. Why do you need to twist and distort the truth about the Catholic Church to sell your message? How successful would your ministry be if you had to tell the truth 100% of the time? Why are you so angry with the Catholic Church that you attack it with lies and distortions? G.S., Internet

Response

I do not undervalue church history or some teachings and traditions of church leaders, but the Scriptures are far more authoritative. The former may err, but the latter can never err. I think you would agree there is no higher authority than our almighty God and Creator, and He has revealed Himself through His Word. "All Scripture is inspired by God and profitable for teaching, reproof, correction, and instruction in righteousness" (2 Timothy 3:16). It should be clear from this verse that Scripture is the final court of appeals for correcting any man's teaching or tradition. Anyone who does not teach in conformity to the authority of Scripture is said to have no light in them (Isaiah 8:20). It is the Word of God, not the words of "infallible" popes, that will judge you on the last day (John 12:48). Regarding the ungodly practice of indulgences, Martin Luther denounced the selling of them in 1517, which ignited the Protestant Reformation. The Catholic Church "teaches and commands that the usage of indulgences, a usage most beneficial to Christians and approved by the authority of the Sacred Council, should be kept in the Church; and it condemns with anathema those who say that indulgences are useless or that the Church does not have the power to grant them" (Vatican II, "The Constitution on the Sacred Liturgy"). The most common practice of indulgences occurs when Catholics pay a priest to offer the Sacrifice of the Mass for a deceased family member.

This is said to reduce their time in purgatory. According to Catholic authorities, you do this by placing an offering in an envelope with your intentions for the Mass and then handing the envelope to the priest who lays it on the altar as he offers the Mass. The required offering varies according to the type of Mass that is requested (www.knocknovena.com). I verified this by calling several Catholic priests.

Ignorance of Catholicism

I am a Catholic who is well educated with a minor in theology. You know nothing of Catholicism except the lies you have been taught. You are the ones deceived. My Church was founded by Christ; yours was founded by a human. You are unable to interpret the scriptures properly because you are prejudiced by the Protestant Tradition (invented in the 1500's). The Catholic Church doesn't teach that those who depend on performing good works, or adhering to a religious system, can be saved. This is a lie that you were told. The Catholic Church has ALWAYS taught salvation by GRACE alone. You may be surprised, but the main function of the pope is to insure that nothing is added or deleted from both the Bible (written Tradition) and Oral Tradition. The Catholic Church is the only church which takes the Bible seriously. I'm sorry that you've been so brainwashed with your protestant traditions that you refuse to submit to the teachings of the Bible. The Bible was written by Catholics. It's obvious you don't take the Bible seriously, because if you did it would bring you into the Catholic Church. Either the Catholic Church is the Bride of Christ or it is the Whore of Babylon. It cannot be somewhere in between. I trust in God, you trust in men. In Christ Jesus and Mary, D.R., Internet

Response

Personal bias and prejudice are difficult to set aside when one's religious faith is involved. So we must examine facts objectively. Be careful what you accept as truth. My knowledge of Catholicism comes from its official teachings. From your comments,

I wonder if you have read the *New Catechism of the Catholic Church*. Paragraph 1821 states: "Each one of us should hope... to obtain the joy of heaven, as God's eternal reward for the *good works accomplished* with the grace of Christ." According to the Bible, heaven is not a reward but a gift, and it is through faith and not by works (Ephesians 2:8–9). In fact, if you mix works with grace, as this paragraph suggests, grace is no longer grace (Romans 11:6). You are correct, Rome has always taught salvation by grace alone, but not through faith alone; therefore the Catholic concept of grace is not the Bible's concept of grace. God's grace is *unmerited*. It does not flow from the side of Christ, through the hands of Mary, and through the sacraments. It is not earned as described in paragraph 2027: "We can *merit* for ourselves and for others the graces needed to attain eternal life." If the Pope's main function is to ensure nothing is deleted from the Bible, you might want to inform him that he approved the deletion of the 2nd Commandment of God from page 496 of the new Catechism. When I took the Bible seriously I left the Catholic Church, never to return to a system that deceives its people concerning the most critical issue of their lives—how can sinners be reconciled to a holy God?

No Salvation Outside the Catholic Church

I was quite saddened when I found your website. While I am not as learned as you are, I do know there is no salvation outside the Catholic Church. I looked into many Christian denominations before looking closely at the Catholic Church. I found things here that others can only imagine. I will pray for you and the many souls you are leading down the wrong path. The Catholic Church is the Church established by Christ. J.C., Internet

Response

The Bible does not teach that belonging to a certain church is necessary for salvation. Nor does it teach that a church has the power to save anyone. Salvation is a free gift! Only those who are born-again of the Holy Spirit become members of the one true church, which is the Body of Christ (Ephesians 5:23b, 1 Corinthians 12:13).

Who Has The Truth?

There are millions of Christians who interpret scriptures differently than you do. Who is right? Who has the real truth? Saying that you are right and the rest of the world's Christians are wrong is not acceptable. M.L., Internet

Response

I have never said I am right; in fact, I never ask people to believe as I believe, but to believe only what God has revealed through His written Word. I point people to the Scriptures, which are able to make them "wise onto salvation." As the Holy Spirit illuminates their minds and hearts they will find the narrow road that leads to eternal life (Matthew 7:13–14). The misinterpretation of Scripture has been the cause of much division within professing Christianity. The Apostle Paul gave this exhortation: "Be diligent to present yourself approved to God as a workman who does not need to be ashamed, handling accurately the word of truth" (2 Timothy 2:15). In order to gain an accurate interpretation of the Bible (or any other book) we must follow some basic principles of interpretation. We must take God's Word literally unless the author or speaker uses figurative expressions in the form of parables, metaphors, or similes. We must look for the author's intended meaning and purpose (in the original language) both to the immediate as well as future audiences. We must consider the context. Is the verse consistent with the theme and purpose of the book? Is it consistent with the full counsel of God's Word? Scripture never contradicts Scripture. However, there may be perceived contradictions because our finite minds cannot fully comprehend the mind of God. However, this should motivate a devoted follower of Jesus Christ to dig deeper, using Scripture to interpret Scripture. It is also wise to avoid establishing a doctrine based on an obscure passage of Scripture. Ultimately we will all be responsible for our own interpretation of God's Word. Most of the New Testament was written to Christians (not to a group of bishops who declare themselves to be the only infallible interpreters of the Bible). We must follow the example of the Bereans who were commended for examining the Scriptures daily to see if what the Apostle Paul said was true (Acts 17:11). Since Paul, who was the most prolific writer of the New Testament, came under the scrutiny of Scripture, everyone who teaches or interprets God's Word must come under the same scrutiny. Anyone who blindly accepts the interpretation of another, without studying the passage for themselves, can be deceived and not even know it. Yes, there are some difficult passages in the Bible that require a deeper level of study, but the majority of Scripture can be easily understood by those who turn from other mediators to the Lord Jesus (2 Corinthians 3:16). Paul's writings were a "manifestation of truth...to every man's conscience in the sight of God" (2 Corinthians 4:2). We must use various disciplines of grammar, literary criticism, historical studies, historical theology, biblical theology, and systematic theology. Only then can we know what the text says, what the text means, and how the text applies personally.

Apostasy

I was deeply saddened to find your web page. It is one of many mediums Satan uses to deceive people and to lead them out of the one true Church. I am writing out of charity and in service to God because if you continue in your ways, you will find yourselves accountable to Christ when He returns. Your article on apostasy states that, "Apostates deny the sufficiency of Christ's atonement." Well, by that definition, St. Paul was an apostate: "Now I rejoice in my sufferings for your sake, and in my flesh I complete what is lacking in Christ's afflictions for the sake of His Body, that is, the Church" (Colossians 1:24). I will pray for you that you might see the error in your ways. R.M., Internet

Response

We will all be held accountable to the Lord Jesus and His Word when He returns. Surely you would agree that you cannot improve upon perfection by adding anything to it, let alone more suffering. The atonement of Christ is sufficient to make *perfect forever* all who believe the gospel (Hebrews 10:10–14). The suffering Paul refers to is for the sake of the body of Christ and for the proclamation of the gospel. Those who follow Jesus will suffer and be persecuted (2 Timothy 3:11). Thus, in the passage you refer to, Paul suffers for Christ's sake and for the sake of "the body."

Temporal Punishment

Jesus died so we do not have to suffer from eternal punishment, but if you're saying He also died to pay all temporal punishments, why do women have pain in childbirth? These are all effects of temporal punishment, due to original sin. If Jesus' death and resurrection eliminated those, why are they still there? M. P., Internet

Response

There is a difference between consequences of sin and punishment for sin. The wages of sin is death (Romans 6:23). The second death is the eternal lake of fire where the wrath of God is poured out on those who rejected His only provision for their sin (Revelation 20:13–15). Jesus saves repenting sinners from the penalty, power, and (eventually) the presence of sin, not from sin's consequences in this world. Your catechism teaches indulgences are the remission of the temporal punishment due to sin (para. 1471). According to your logic, a Catholic could apply indulgences to the pains of childbirth and they would cease to exist.

Unequally Yoked

I am a Christian who, a little over a year ago, married into a very devout and deeply-rooted Catholic family. My heart aches for my husband who is still a Catholic, because I know that, should his life be taken, his destiny is the eternal lake of fire. I have very little room to verbally witness to him. I pray daily and often that God will continue to mercifully spare his life in hopes he will become a true believer. I knew when I married him that a believer is not to be unequally yoked. At the time I was not walking with the Lord as I should have been, but that is forgiven and now my heart is burdened beyond explanation for him. I cannot bear to think that when life ends we will be forever separated. Please, if you can help me in some way, I would be so grateful. Anonymous, Internet

Response

My heart also grieves for those who refuse to turn to Christ and His Word because they are so blinded by religious deception. Continue to pray diligently for him until his heart is ready to receive the gospel. Sow the seed of God's imperishable Word whenever you are led to do so by the Holy Spirit. I encourage you to read and apply 1 Peter 3:1–6 and Colossians 4:2–6. Let him witness your joy and peace as you become the wife Christ wants you to be. May God comfort you as you trust His promises.

How Can I be Excommunicated?

Recently I made a request to be excommunicated from the Catholic Church. Unfortunately, after two letters to my former priest, there was no response. He did not even attempt to deter me from my course despite the fact that according to cannon laws 750 & 751, I cannot be saved once I refuse to remain within the "one holy Catholic Church." Considering I spent much of my teenage years working closely with him at the church rectory, his complete lack of concern for me really grieves me. Since he did not respond, I took matters into my own hands and called up the Archdiocese of Chicago. The receptionist rather combatively told me, "You just can't be excommunicated. If you aren't willing to practice your faith, that's a private matter; we don't have any documents of that kind!" When pressed further she became downright antagonistic and referred me to the chancellor's office. There they were cordially willing to allow me to slip into "damnation" without even an attempt to warn me of my "impending doom!" Within two days they sent me notification that my request had been granted. May the Lord use this incident as an educating tool for your readers who may be interested in doing the same thing. It is good to know that you are sticking up for the truth of God's amazing grace without fear of censure. V.D. Kenosha, WI

Response
Thank you for sharing this letter. It gives people an insight into the "fruit of Rome." This is one of the reasons why Roman Catholicism boasts of having over 1 billion members.

Sacrament Necessary for Salvation
Where in the Catechism does it say that Catholics need the sacraments to get to heaven? I am trying hard to understand your motives for lying. Every time you attack and claim that my church is antibiblical you are showing your ignorance. The Bible is the cornerstone of our religious education, and our spiritual lives. How would Jesus look upon you and your followers? You are spending your time creating a rift with fellow Christians. Why do you continue to lie about the Catholic Church? I will continue to pray for you and hope that you see the light. I pray that you will stop spreading untruths and hurt and start really doing God's will. S. S. Internet

Response
Paragraph 1129 of *The Catechism of the Catholic Church* states: "The Church affirms that for believers the sacraments of the Covenant are necessary for salvation." If you really believed the Jesus of the Bible you would not participate in a religious system that denies His atonement is sufficient for your salvation. Penitent sinners are "justified as a gift by His grace through the

redemption which is in Christ Jesus (not sacraments); whom God displayed publicly as a propitiation in His blood through faith" (Romans 3:24–25). If you were obedient to the Scriptures you would withdraw yourself from Catholic clergy who teach doctrines contrary to the words of Jesus Christ (1 Timothy 6:3–5).

Thirty Thousand Denominations

Jesus said that He came to build His Church. Which one of the 30,000 Protestant churches do you think He was talking about? Protestants say that they only need the Bible and yet you all believe differently. How is that unity? Dawn, Internet

Response

Christ's church is made up of all who have been called by the Father and sealed by the Holy Spirit upon repenting and believing the gospel of Jesus Christ. They are called "saints" because He has saved them completely, having obtained their eternal redemption by shedding His blood to cover their sins. They were baptized by one Spirit into one body, which is the church (1 Corinthians 12:13). The physical building where people worship or their denominational affiliation does not determine membership in the true church. There are many within both Catholic and Protestant churches who profess Christ, but do not possess Him. You are correct, there are apostate Protestant churches also. However, churches have certain freedoms within Scripture to develop forms and structures in harmony with biblical principles and yet, at the same time, be culturally relevant. Everyone born of God believes the same gospel. It is in the Gospel of Jesus Christ where all believers are united, not in forms and liturgies.

Salvation by Faith Plus Works

I am struggling with the question of salvation for those who believe that works must be added to the cross-work of Christ. Even my sister, who is right-on about most things regarding the faith, believes that, as long as the foundation is Christ and the cross, none of the rest matters. (She got this mindset from a Billy Graham interview on TV. He believes Catholics are saved because their foundation is in Christ). My prayer continues to be that God will strip away all the wrong beliefs I may be adhering to so that all that is left is the doctrines of God in their purest form. Can you shed some Biblical light on this matter? As always I appreciate you and your heart in this ministry. The more Catholics I encounter the more I respect what you and Jane have committed to do through PTG. M. C. Plano, TX

Response

The Scriptures reveal that good works and God's grace are mutually exclusive in justification. Those who believe good works are necessary to be justified remain condemned. Grace is the only means by which God saves sinners (Romans 11:6). For the gift of eternal life to be possessed, it must be received with empty hands of faith. Works are the demonstration of salvation given by God's grace after justification (Ephesians 2:8–10). Spiritually dead people can only do works in the flesh, which are like filthy rags to God (Isaiah 64:6). "They that are in the flesh cannot please God" (Romans 8:8). From God's perspective, "there is none that does good, no, not one" (Romans 3:12). One must be born of the Spirit of God through faith in order to do good works that please God. We are not saved by righteous works, but by God's mercy (Titus 3:5). Once we are regenerated it is no longer we who live, but Christ who lives through us (Galatians 2:20). We must then be "zealous of good works" and "learn to engage in good deeds" (Titus 2:14; 3:14). When we receive rewards in heaven we give them back to Christ, for it was He living through us who actually earned them (Revelation 4:10).

Your Ministry is Deceptive

I am a Catholic, and attend a Catholic university where I am working on my Masters in Theology. I do not have time to scan every word of your immense website, but I am very disappointed with the misinformation you provide. I have yet to find a Protestant who actually knows the Catholic faith and uses truth in their conversion attempts. Your site leaves me with the feeling that you believed the lies, and now you participate in their dissemination. I call on you to repent of this deception before it's too late. Larisa, Internet

Response
You are like so many Catholics who accuse me of disseminating lies about their church, yet never offer even one example. It is my desire to objectively present a comparison of what I believe to be the heretical teachings of your Catholic Catechism in light of God's holy Word so that Catholics will repent of their dead works and believe the gospel. Whenever I point out an error in Catholic teaching, I quote directly from the source with paragraph numbers and contrast them with Scripture references. If you find one instance where I have misrepresented the official teachings of your church, I will apologize and correct my mistake.

Lack of Discernment
I have been a Baptist for 20 years now and find it hard to believe that the very religion we "branched off from" could be this horrid cult you make it out to be. I honestly cannot see any difference in the two religions. It's time we stop bashing other religions and start trying to learn from them. B.S., Internet

Response
The differences between Catholicism and the gospel are as great as the differences between heaven and hell. An example is the dogmas of indulgences and purgatory. How can Catholics earn or pay for indulgences in light of Psalm 49:7–8? And how can purgatory purge sin in light of Hebrews 1:3; 1 John 1:7, and Colossians 1:22? Furthermore, the Catholic Church condemns everyone who believes they are saved by faith alone in Christ alone by grace alone. Those examples alone are substantial differ-

ences. It is not bashing someone to point out fatal flaws in their belief system.

Salvation by Keeping the Law

I am someone who may be a "recovering Catholic" and need an answer to a question that has been bothering me. If keeping the Law is not the basis for salvation, why did Jesus tell the rich man to keep the commandments when he asked Him how to get into heaven? I apologize for my lack of the specific verse, but remember I am Catholic. M. D., Internet

Response

The passage you are referring to is Luke 18:18–29. Remember, whenever we interpret a verse we must always look at the context. The rich man was looking for something he could *do* to be assured of eternal life. Jesus took him to the law in an effort to convict him of his sin and his need for a savior. When he wasn't convicted of his sin, Jesus gave him a good work to do, sell everything and give it to the poor. Those who heard Jesus recognized the sheer impossibility of anyone ever doing enough good works to qualify for heaven. Jesus reveals our only hope of eternal life is to trust what God has done for us, not what man can do for God. In Luke 18:27 Jesus says, "What is impossible with man is possible with God." Salvation is of the Lord from beginning to end (Philippians 1:6). In other words, our only hope is to cease from trusting in our own righteousness and rely solely on Christ's righteousness (2 Corinthians 5:21; Philippians 3:9). That perfect righteousness is credited to a repentant sinner at the moment he receives Christ through faith (Romans 4:5).

Works are the Evidence of Salvation

Christians do good works, just like Catholics, but what is the difference? I need to get this topic straight. Faith with no works is "useless" (James 2:20) and "dead" (James 2:17), so is there a clear-cut reason why we do God's work? When do good works become not as a result of salvation, but rather as a reason to be further justified? E.C., Cerritos, CA

Response

The difference is found in Ephesians 2:10. Those who have been born of God will do works that God has prepared for them. Prior to being born again, we are spiritually dead (Ephesians 2:1) and any works we do are filthy rags in God's sight (Isaiah 64:6). James is addressing those who profess Christ, but lack any evidence (works) of being converted. James wrote: "You see then that a man is justified by works and not by faith alone" (James 2:24). The Greek word for "justify" also means "to vindicate, to defend, or uphold." So James is saying: "You see then that a man is vindicated (upholds his living faith) by his works and not merely by a profession of faith." The word "vindicate" could also mean to clear from criticism or suspicion. In no way is James teaching that sinners are justified by works because he has already made the point that salvation is a gift from God according to His will, not the will of man (1:17–18). James is asking professing Christians, who have not shown evidence of their new life in Christ, to "show me your faith" (James 2:18). But faith is invisible to man. It is an unseen relationship between man and God. Since faith cannot be seen, the best way to prove one's faith is to be "doers of the Word and not merely hearers" (James 1:22). Those who do the Word of God will desire to live a righteous life in obedience to God. That is why James said: "I will show you my faith by my works" (James 2:18). James is saying that justifying faith will be evidenced by works. Only genuine faith is alive and bears fruit. The presence of fruit on a tree reveals whether the tree is alive or dead. Faith alone justifies, but faith that justifies is never alone. James is saying that dead faith cannot justify anyone and it is useless (James 2:20). We cannot add to Christ's perfect work of redemption. Any attempt to do so nullifies God's grace. Once Jesus saves us, we do the works God has prepared for us out of love and appreciation. Christians do good works because Jesus saved them. According to the *New Catholic Catechism*, Catholics do works to merit their salvation.

Sheep Stealing

Since born-again Christians "evangelize" Catholics or "steal sheep" from the Catholic Church, why shouldn't the Catholic Church also "evangelize" or "steal sheep" away from Protestant churches? Some Catholics may become Christians, but can Christians become Catholics? E. C., Internet

Response

A Catholic can become a Christian only when the true Shepherd calls and he/she repents and believes the gospel. A Christian following Christ will not follow the voice of a stranger whose underlying motive is to deceive and kill (John 10). It is difficult for Catholics to steal sheep because they have no good news to attract them. A born-again Christian has the assurance of eternal life, the complete forgiveness of sins, and a permanent right standing before God. Catholicism does not offer these spiritual blessings.

True Love Loves Truth

I know that Jesus would not want me bashing other religions, but rather to seek to understand and to love our fellow brothers on earth enough to respect what they stand for. Jesus would not want us fighting amongst ourselves, but rather living out His Word. Spreading untruths and hurting others by insulting their faith is the work of the devil. E. K., Internet

Response

How well do you know the Jesus of the Bible? Have you read that He came to earth "not to bring peace, but a sword...to set a man against his father, and a daughter against her mother?" If you were a disciple of Jesus you would rebuke false religious leaders as He did for shutting the kingdom of God in men's faces. Have you read the terrible "woes" Jesus gave to false teachers in Matthew 23:13–36? Do you know that God hates what is false (Psalm 119:104)? Christians are also to hate what is false (Proverbs 13:5) The doctrines of purgatory and indulgences are not only false, they rob Christ of His glory and devalue His precious blood that was shed to purify sin. Until you come to the Scriptures with a broken and contrite heart, seeking Jesus as He is revealed, you may never find the narrow gate that leads to eternal life.

I Was Born a Catholic and I Will Die a Catholic

I could no more renounce my Catholic faith than I could gouge out my eyes! What type of people are you? You have no idea what Christ teaches! Love comes from within. If only you realized the contempt that your pithy insults breed! I am a proud Catholic who is also proud to say that he respects all religions that seek peace in love. I am offended by your insults! Turn away from your path of hate, it will lead to everlasting torment! C. H., Internet

Response

The fact that you respect all religions that seek peace and love is an indication that you do not know what Christ taught. He was intolerant of any other way to the Father (John 14:6). Jesus said, "I am the gate; whoever enters through Me will be saved" (John 10:9). He said, "Enter through the narrow gate. For wide is the gate and broad is the road that leads to destruction, and many enter through it" (Matthew 7:13). The wide road is marked "to heaven" (by Satan), but it leads to judgment. It is traveled by all the religions of the world that believe in a works-righteousness system of salvation. True love does not come from within; it comes from God. It is a love that proclaims the truth and hates what is false. It has a compassion for deceived people and points them to the narrow gate for salvation.

Who is Deceiving Whom?

I have viewed your website and am amazed with the utter lack of truth in it. It is clear you were never a real student of Catholicism. You tell poor unsuspecting people the RCC teaches that the sacrifice of Jesus was not enough to redeem mankind. This is a total and complete lie. In fact the Church teaches that the Incarnation of Christ alone would have been sufficient to redeem mankind. So now that you know this, will you change the erroneous info on your web page? I doubt it because you are not committed to the truth. Khaled, Internet

Response

The Incarnation of Christ alone would NOT have been sufficient to redeem mankind. Have you not read: "without the shedding of blood there is no forgiveness of sins" (Hebrews 9:22)? Repenting sinners can only be reconciled to God through faith in the death and resurrection of Christ (Colossians 1:22). "We have redemption through his blood, the forgiveness of sins, in accordance with the riches of God's grace" (Ephesians 1:7). Furthermore, if Christ was not raised from the dead then our faith is useless (1 Corinthians15:14). If your church proclaimed the true gospel you would know that the death and resurrection of Jesus according to the Scriptures are necessary for man's redemption (1 Corinthians 15:1–4). Now that you know the biblical truth, will you seek a church that teaches it?

The True Church

We are the true church because Jesus gave the keys to the Kingdom of Heaven to Peter alone (Matthew 16:19). We know the apostles believed their office was to pass on to their successors (Acts 1:15–26). I choose to follow the Church that traces her history back to the apostles. Besides, I have everything in the Catholic Church—the Trinity, the Eucharist, His Blessed Mother, purgatory, etc. Oh, the glory of it all! Mart W., Internet

Response

Actually Jesus gave the keys to all His disciples (Matthew 18:18). The keys could very well be a figurative expression for the gospel, which opens the gates of heaven to all who believe. If you look closely at Acts 1:15–26 you will note a very distinctive requirement for apostolic succession. The successor must have been a witness of the earthly ministry of Jesus, from His baptism through His resurrection (Acts 1:21). None of your so-called "successors" of Peter ever met this requirement. Did you know the apostles replaced Judas because he was an apostate (Acts 1:25)? It is interesting to see how the RCC has followed Judas into apostasy, even to the extent of replacing its apostate popes and bishops.

Which Authority is Supreme?

You are so misinformed it is pathetic. You don't even have a clue as to what Catholics believe. It is really sad. I have the authority of Christ's Church. Protestant sects have nothing. I know the Church back to front. I have loved the Church since I was born. Your website is spreading lies about Christ's teachings. Anyone who is sincere in following the good that has been revealed to them can enter Christ's Kingdom. Joe, Internet

Response

You are right in saying I don't have a clue what Catholics believe, but I do know what they are taught. It is for this reason we persuade Catholics to be good Bereans, that is, to test every teaching with the Scriptures (Acts 17:11). When you do this you will find it is the Catholic Catechism that is spreading lies about Christ's teaching. If you knew the Bible from "back to front" you would discover Scripture has authority over the church (2 Timothy 3:16). You would also see that many sincere people will be barred from the kingdom of heaven (Matthew 23:13–14). Why are you so hostile towards me? "Have I now become your enemy by telling you the truth" (Galatians 4:16)?

The sign of real hatred is when those who know the gospel remain silent while the population of hell continues to grow.

Apostolic or Apostate

How can all you Protestants be right when you have over 20,000 denominations and churches? You must come back to Holy Mother Church to experience the true faith and the fullness of salvation. M. G., Metarie, LA

Response

There are really only two churches. One is apostolic and includes all who have been baptized of the Holy Spirit (1 Corinthians 12:13). The other is apostate and is made up of those who name Christ, but compromise His gospel. Yes, there are many divisions among professing Christians, but this is sometimes an indication of the Holy Spirit's work. Whenever a church begins to depart from the apostolic faith, true believers will separate from the apostates. This is what occurred during the Reformation, and still continues today. Doctrinal differences over the content of the gospel necessitate division. True believers are called to walk in the light and have nothing to do with the works of darkness (2 Corinthians 6:14–18). May God help you to see the light of the gospel and the glory of Christ!

Salvation by Another Name

How can you say Catholics need to be saved? By virtue of their Catholic faith they are heaven bound. Elizabeth B., Internet

Response

The Apostle Peter, whom you Catholics believe was the first pope, said there is no other name under heaven by which we can be saved (Acts 4:12). Your Catholic faith cannot save you. The Jewish faith could not save Paul. He exchanged his religion for an eternal relationship with God (Philippians 3:4–10). No one can enter God's kingdom unless they are born "again" or born "from above" (John 3:3). This new birth is supernatural and is entirely an act of God that results in eternal life. It contains no human element, nor does it lie within the scope of human achievement (John 1:13). If you continue to trust the traditions of men you will never understand the sovereign grace of God.

Hateful Attacks

It is unfortunate that you feel that you must attack the Catholic Church. It is this type of hate that spews forth and divides people. You seem afraid of the truth. Remember tradition has always been the root of the Catholic Church. Before you bash Jesus and His teachings try reading and asking questions that can be answered in the *Catechism of the Catholic Church*. Otherwise you are an unadvised messenger of the devil. Patricia B., Internet

Response

Is it hate when you stand on the broad road that leads to destruction and point people to the narrow gate that leads to life? Is it hate when you tell people who are paying for indulgences to get their relatives out of purgatory that there is no purgatory? When one billion souls trust a pope dressed in gold and fine linen and his religious rituals and you tell them they need only Jesus—is this hate? When Jesus rebuked the religious leaders of His day and called them "snakes and vipers" for deceiving His people—was this hate? I pray that you would see that true hatred is when you allow loved ones to march proudly towards hell's gate without confronting them with the truth that can save them. True love loves truth! To free a man from the bondage of deception, you must first show him that he is deceived.

Do you Think we are Stupid?

It is a shame that you persist in spreading lies and falsehoods about Catholics! And the shame is on you! What you are doing is spreading deception. You must think your readers are stupid or would not consult Catholic sources for what we believe! You might make the poor peasant believe your lies and falsehoods, but sooner or later he will hear the truth! Mike W., Internet

Response

Our publications quote official Catholic sources verbatim and our website is linked to many Catholic authoritative sites so that everyone can see how Catholic teachings violate biblical integrity. Truth always exposes error just as light dispels darkness!

Pleasantly Surprised

I heard about your site in a Yahoo chat room. I was pleasantly surprised because I am a Catholic who never learned how to follow the Lord, or who He is. I printed out some of your information and stuck it on our Church bulletin board. When I approached my priest with my concerns, he became indignant and even hostile. I'll probably get excommunicated now. I was so happy to see the truth on your website that will correct my wrong beliefs. Most Catholics go to church because it's a duty, and not because they truly love the Lord. I want to thank you for trying to alert fellow Catholics. K.G., Ossining, NY

Response

We praise God for granting you repentance leading to a knowledge of the truth. Let us know how we can serve you.

Business or Ministry?

It is obvious by your website that you treat Christianity as a business, not a religion. To get "customers" you market a cheap ripoff of Christ's message by using misinterpreted Biblical passages. You show that salvation can be attained by a meaningless declaration. This creates a larger market and larger profits. For me, I am satisfied with my Catholic faith. It gives me a sense that I am in control of my salvation and challenges me to earn it. I do not give in to those who want to profit on my beliefs. I sincerely hope that you change the message of this site that shamelessly is out to make a cheap buck out of your deceived "market share." Pete, Internet

Response

I neither treat Christianity as either a religion or a business, but as a cherished relationship with God through Jesus Christ. If you will investigate our website objectively, you will see that our mission is to set captives free from the bondage of religion and sin. We do this by proclaiming the truth of God's Word (John 8:31–32). Nowhere on our site, or in the Scriptures, will you find anyone attaining salvation by meaningless declarations. On the contrary, you will find that salvation is entirely a work of God. Only those who see it as such can begin to understand His grace and mercy. Religious pride often keeps people from coming to God with broken, contrite hearts to receive His free gift of eternal life. Instead they boast of being in control of their eternal destiny and earning what God gives freely. Regarding your criticism that our ministry is seeking a larger profit, this is also unfounded. We send out tens of thousands of our publications free of charge. We trust our sovereign Lord, who faithfully meets all our needs through those who share our compassion and burden for the lost.

Leaving Tracts on Cars at Catholic Churches

I question the fruit of your labor in leaving flyers on everyone's car while they are attending Mass. Is our faith so scary that you feel you must try to abolish it? Your publications suggest Catholics can "buy" their way into heaven through purgatory and indulgences. This is not true. How can Galatians condemn the Catholic gospel when it was the Catholic Church who canonized the gospel? Besides, the gospel of grace is without a doubt a false doctrine. Stop listening to your crazy cult leaders. They are leading you astray. Study the teachings of the Church Fathers. J. G., Garland

Response

Placing gospel tracts in places where the lost will read them is indeed a fruitful way of calling God's elect out of spiritual darkness into the glorious light of His Son. If you dare to read the Vatican Council II documents you will see your church acknowledges the collection of "profits" from those who were trying to buy their way into heaven with indulgences. The Book of Galatians condemns the Catholic gospel as it did the Judaizer's gospel for nullifying God's grace with works. If you study the teachings of the apostles rather than the church fathers you will see God saves sinners by grace, and gives eternal life as a gift to those who come to the cross with empty hands of faith (Ephesians 2:8–9).

Born-Again Catholic?

My fiancée is a born-again Catholic. I've told him that I don't want to raise my children in a Catholic church. Please pray that he'll be willing to break away from tradition and from the Catholic church so that he can grow in his relationship with Christ. If this doesn't happen, I must call off the wedding. Besides Jesus and my mother, he's my best friend, but I must be obedient to Jesus Christ. M.S., Elkview, WV

Response

You are right for not wanting to be unequally yoked in marriage with a Catholic (2 Corinthians 6:14). A born-again Catholic is an oxymoron. Everyone who is born of God will repent of the false gospel that he or she once embraced and will believe that Jesus is sufficient to save them completely and forever. It is impossible for anyone to believe two opposing gospels at the same time. Please go to our website to download the "Oxymoron" article so you can share it with him. If he is unwilling to leave, it is a good indication that he does not have the Spirit of truth indwelling him.

Purgatory is a Jewish Tradition

I was born a Catholic, then left the church to join the Christian fundamentalist church, the "born-agains." I found out that they are not the original Christians, but a dividing factor in the body of Christ. Jesus established the Catholic Church with Saint Peter as the head. Your preaching deceives and manipulates people's minds. Your rebellion and lack of understanding of the genuine Bible (put together in the 5th century by the Catholics) is your failure. Faith alone is not enough to save you. Purgatory is a Jewish tradition where we pay our debt, because sin is a debt. We Catholics adopted that tradition because we are Judeo-Christians. I am willing to debate you and to prove you wrong. E. Garcia, Internet

Response

Let us reason together with the Scriptures. God appointed Jesus to be head over everything for the Church (Ephesians 1:22). The Church He established is not the Roman Catholic Church, but the church made up of those whose names are written in heaven (Hebrews 12:23). True Christians, those who follow Jesus, may be divisive because Jesus came to divide believers from unbelievers, even among family members (Matthew 10:34–38). It matters not when the Bible was put together, what matters is that all Scripture is inspired by God at the moment the pen made contact with the original manuscripts. Purgatory is actually a pagan tradition that some Jews followed, however God's Word tells us: "No man can redeem the life of another or give to God a ransom for him, the ransom for a life is costly, no payment is ever enough" (Psalm 49:7–8). There is really nothing to be gained in debating you. You are convinced you are right and God has already called me through His gospel and the sanctifying work of His Spirit.

Out of Darkness Into Light

When you spoke at my church last weekend you made a big impact on me, helping me to see things clearly. After listening to you I realized I was one of those you referred to, who liked to be in the darkness. I was having too much fun in my sin and didn't want to give it up. I would like to become a born-again Christian. I was brought up going to church, but lost contact with God as I got older. I want to know what I should do, is it too late? I also want to be able to minister to my Catholic family and to my friends. I plan on asking my pastor for some guidance. But any little thing that you can say or any little prayer that you would say for me would be greatly appreciated. Please help me. Initials Withheld, Weatherford, OK

Response

I praise God that He has called you to repentance through the preaching of His Word! May I now encourage you to read Psalm 51:1–17, which is a contrite sinner's prayer for pardon. Then call upon the Lord Jesus to save you from the punishment and power of your sins. Everyone who beholds the Son and believes in Him has eternal life (John 6:40). I will pray for you and send you some publications that will help you grow in the grace and knowledge of Jesus.

Reasons Why you Left the True Church

I recently received two of your tracts and your newsletter. The darkness that has enveloped your mind so completely is frightening to behold. Not content to live alone in that awful darkness, you insist on seeking out others to reside there with you. Choosing error for yourself is one thing; forcing error upon others is another matter entirely, a terribly grave one. I was forced to contemplate just why you felt compelled to produce such utter nonsense. There could be several reasons: (1) you're lying, and never were in fact a Catholic and always have been a mere Protestant; (2) someone within the Catholic Church, a priest or perhaps a nun, hurt you in a profound, deep, emotional way, driving you from the Church; (3) maybe the priests simply failed to properly instruct you in the Faith; or (4) perhaps you're terribly gullible, dim-witted, and prone to believing anything some two-bit tent preacher yells at you before asking for a donation. Had you been properly taught true Catholic theology, you wouldn't have experienced a mid-life crisis and gone lusting after the simple and empty pleasures of the harlot known as Protestantism. It is an intellectually dead vacuum, a one-way trip to Theological Neverland. J.S., Marion, NC

Response

You are right on the mark when you accuse me of "producing such utter nonsense." It comes directly from the *Catechism of the Catholic Church*, which I quote verbatim. So often, when Catholics are unable to refute the objective facts I present, they either resort to concocting reasons why I left the Catholic religion or attack my character. The reason I left, and now serve my Lord in this ministry, is because God has shone His light in my heart to give me the knowledge of His glory (2 Corinthians 4:6). One of the great paradoxes is how two sinners can read the same gospel tract and be impacted so differently. One responds by seeking the Savior's mercy while the other rejects the gift of salvation because he is blinded by his pride and self-righteousness. "God is opposed to the proud but gives grace to the humble" (James 4:6).

You Have Made Me More Devout

You have encouraged me to become a more devout Catholic. Because of you and your ministry, I go to Mass everyday and I have placed all my trust in God through the Immaculate Heart of Mary. I know that true faith is in the Catholic Church. Faith is not only believing in God and all that He has said, but also believing in all that the Catholic Church proposes for our belief. Therefore, true faith comes to us through the Catholic Church. This means that apart from the Catholic Church, the fullness of salvation is not easily obtained. But those who through no fault of their own do not know Christ or His Church may still be saved if they have a sincere heart and try to do God's will as they know it through their conscience. But those, like yourself, who, knowing that the Catholic Church was founded by Christ, would refuse to enter it or remain in it cannot be saved. There is nothing in the teachings of the Catholic Church opposed to Sacred Scripture. I will pray for you and ask Mary, the

Queen of the Universe, to pray for you. I will offer up your soul to Her Immaculate Heart that she may present it, perfect and blameless, before God. My faith in Her has been strengthened because of what God has done through you. Your ministry is inspired by Satan, and I will pray that you convert and believe in the truth some day. Michael T., Internet

Response

In your brief letter you have inadvertently but actually affirmed four of the many ways Catholic doctrines oppose Sacred Scripture. You have falsely trusted God through Mary, because Jesus is the only mediator between man and God (1 Timothy 2:5). You and your church fail to realize that true faith is "the faith" that was once and for all delivered to the saints in the first century and does not include the ungodly dogmas of indulgences, purgatory, and the bloodless ritual of the Mass (Jude 3). You and your church also fail to realize there is no salvation apart from Jesus, for His blood alone is necessary to atone for sin (Acts 4:12). Finally, it is Jesus, not Mary, who is able to present me blameless before God (Jude 24). One of the clever strategies of the devil is to appeal to man's senses by mixing a little error with truth (Genesis 3:1–7). He has outwitted you because you are unaware of his schemes (2 Corinthians 2:11). If you will turn to Jesus instead of Mary, the veil that blinds you can be removed (2 Corinthians 3:14).

Ex-Catholics are Heretics

It is only the unknowing sheep that follow the wrong shepherd. Why don't you seek faith-filled Roman Catholics instead of preying on those who have lost the faith? How can an ex-Catholic have the faith to understand Jesus when he has left HIS Church. Ex-Catholics are heretics. You should never leave St. Peter because of Judas. Michele, Internet

Response

You are so right! It is only the unknowing sheep who follow the wrong shepherd. They will not know the true Shepherd until God draws them (John 6:44) and they hear the voice of Jesus, the true Shepherd (John 10). There are indeed unknowing sheep in the Catholic Church who blindly follow wolves dressed in sheep's clothing (Matthew 7:14). The purpose of this ministry is to point those lost sheep to the true Shepherd, using His Word, so that they will hear His voice and follow Him. The true Shepherd offers complete forgiveness of sins, His imputed righteousness, and the assurance of eternal life. Your shepherd, the Pope, leads you on the wide road to destruction with his false gospel of works and sacraments and will condemn you with anathemas if you were to ever receive what Jesus offers by grace through faith. The one who is throwing you into confusion will pay the penalty (Galatians 5:10).

Malicious Slander

I hate your ministry and its "godless" aims, since it maliciously slanders Catholics. I feel this ministry insults my intelligence and it makes me sick! Just remember, Mike Gendron, a judgment day is coming, and you will stand before your creator! You will have to answer for rejecting the fullness of His revealed truth as held in both Scripture and Tradition. You will also have to answer for why you twisted His written Word to justify your heretical beliefs, and use it as a hammer against Catholic Christians (2 Peter 1:20; 3:16). You will have to answer for all the insults and blasphemies you have hurled at His precious body and blood, truly present in the Eucharist! You will have to answer for how you neglected His Mother, in defiance of what He said in the commandment, "Thou shall honor (venerate) thy mother and father." The blood of all those who believe your false gospel shall be upon your hands! Indeed, it shall be more tolerable for Sodom and Gommorah during the "Great Judgment" than for you guys! For God shall tell you, "Depart from me, you workers of evil, for I never knew you." Karl M., Internet

Response

It is letters like yours that grieve me to no end. My heart aches for Catholics who allow mediators other than Christ to come between them and God. This leaves them wide open to deception. Our ministry, that you hate, simply points people to Christ and His Word. He is the only Mediator, and the only one who can be trusted. "Cursed is the man who trusts in man…(but) blessed is the man who trusts in the Lord" (Jeremiah 17:5, 7). When I stand before my Creator I will stand washed white as snow by His precious blood. I was once so blind, but He has enabled me to see the glorious truth of His gospel. May He do the same for you!

Mary the Perpetual Virgin

I ask you to convert from your mistaken faith and come into the light and truth of God's Holy Catholic Church. Then you'll know that Mary is the Immaculate Conception, the Co-Redemptrix, and perpetual Virgin. To deny that Mary is all-perfect is to deny all the glory that God deserves. God created Mary as a sinless creature. To refuse to accept Mary as your Mother and Queen is to refuse all that God has done for your redemption. M.T., Internet

Response

Not one of your statements is found in God's holy Word. They are all blasphemous Roman traditions that dishonor the Mary of the Bible and directly contradict the Scriptures. May your zeal be for seeking the truth of God's Word and repenting from anything that opposes it.

Born-Again of Water is Baptism

When Jesus said we must be born again by "water" and the Spirit, He was telling us water baptism is necessary for salvation. What more proof do you need? L. D., San Antonio, TX

Response

Jesus was not referring to water baptism when He spoke of the need to be born again (John 3:5). He was telling Nicodemus that he needed to be born of God because he was spiritually dead. Religious ordinances could not save him. When Jesus spoke of "water" and the Spirit He was referring to the baptism of the Spirit (1 Corinthians 12:13). Water was often used as a symbol of the Holy Spirit (John 7:37–38). John has already stated this new birth cannot be produced by man's will or man's desire, but only by God's will (John 1:12–13). We also know that water baptism does not produce spiritual birth because some Gentiles had received the Holy Spirit prior to being baptized with water (Acts 10:47). The Holy Spirit is received upon believing the gospel, not after a ritual or sacrament has been performed (Ephesians 1:13–14). Paul even called the Galatians foolish for forgetting they had received the Spirit by believing, not by observing the law (Galatians 3:1–2). Water baptism is a profession of faith, and is done in obedience to Christ's great commission after one has been baptized with the Spirit.

Where do I go?

I am a Catholic, but there are many Catholic doctrines I do not believe. I do not believe in purgatory, or in confessing my sins to anyone except God. The only reason I stay in the Catholic Church is my wife of 40 years refuses to leave. I believe that most churches are apostate. What do I do? Steve, Pigeon, MI

Response

God has appointed you to be the spiritual leader of your wife (Ephesians 5:23–27). Lead your wife out of this false religion and find a church where you can worship God in Spirit and Truth (John 4:24). Use the Scriptures and some of our resources to show your wife the fatal errors of Catholicism. Pray for God to grant her repentance leading to a knowledge of the truth (2 Timothy 2:23-25).

Your Catholic Dad is in Heaven

Please do not send me your trash in "Proclaiming The Gospel." I was aghast to hear what you said in your Catholic dad's funeral in the eulogy. You are to be pitied, my friend. I believe your dad is in heaven. If you continue on your path, you will never see him again. You, like many fundamentalist preachers, are preaching only half-truths. I returned to the Catholic Church this year. It was only by the grace of God that He sent a wonderful priest, a teacher, an apologist grounded in Catholic teaching. Did you not know that when your dad was baptized he was promised eternal life with Jesus in heaven? I'm sure that your dad is now praying for your conversion. You are so lost. G.F., Latonsvilles, MD

Response

My dad was promised eternal life by fallible men who refused to share the infallible promises of God's most precious gift with him.

Judge Not

I am a Catholic and more than a little flabbergasted by your web page and "ministry." One of the things I appreciate about the Catholic Church is that it does not judge or condemn other Christians because of their different beliefs. It's a shame that you would waste so much energy on what seems like such a negative effort, convincing people that Catholics are not Christian, condemned, lost, and needing to be "saved." With all the pain and suffering in the world, it's sad that you would make this a priority in your life. You are deceived and I wouldn't want to trade places with you. Patti G., Internet

Response

You must be totally unaware that your church condemns born-again Christians over 100 times for refusing to believe its dogmas. Did you know that spreading the Good News is a responsibility and a privilege that God gave to all Christians?

Opinions vs. Scripture

We all have opinions, but they can't all be right. Why is yours right? What authority does your opinion have? Have you ever tested your beliefs against the early church? Doesn't it make sense to compare your "opinions" of doctrine against the very Fathers who were taught by the apostles? Do you care that your doctrines in the 20th century contradict those of the 1st? Is that really following Christ? Are you believing something Christ did not teach? Dan, Internet

Response

The reason that over 90% of the world's population is deceived and destined for a Christ-less eternity in hell is because they believe man's opinions (teachings and traditions) rather than the Word of God. It is for this reason I avoid sharing my opinions, but rather point people to what is written in the Scriptures. True Christians will use the same authority that Jesus used during His ministry on earth. Three times he rebuked the opinions of Satan with, "It is written" (Matthew 4:1–11). It would be wise for you to answer the questions you have asked of me. Where, in the history of the first century church (the Book of Acts), do you find priests offering sacrifices for sins, people seeking indulgences to remit punishment for their sins, prayers for souls in purgatory, church leaders forbidden to marry, infallible popes, or salvation dispensed through the sacraments? Where do you see rosaries, scapulae, holy water, and statues? The witness of God is greater than the witness of men (1 John 5:9). I suggest you put less emphasis on the early church fathers and more on God's Word. May God's light shine in your heart to give you the knowledge of the glorified Christ!

You Are a Traitor

I read with much sadness your home page information. It is really difficult for me to believe that someone who was a devout Catholic for 34 years could turn traitor on his religious heritage and proclaim such heresy. Are you following Jesus Christ in the only Church He left us? It is not too late for you to save your precious soul, which you have placed in such terrible danger of loss through these heresies that you adhere to and the scandal you cause by posting these. The Scriptures cannot be considered as inerrant; this is a Protestant Fundamentalist mistake. A.K., Internet

Response

By God's grace I heard the voice of the true Shepherd and began following Him. It appears from your comments that you follow your church and its unbiblical teachings rather than Christ. Jesus said His Word is truth (John 17:17). The Scriptures are inerrant because they are the Word of God, and God cannot lie. The men whom God chose to pen the Scriptures could not err in their writings because they were carried along by the Holy Spirit (2 Peter 1:19–21). May God give you the grace to turn to Christ so the veil that covers your heart can be removed (2 Corinthians 3:15–16).

Apostate Baptist Now Catholic

I wrote to you about my decision to become a Catholic and wanted you to know what kind of propaganda I think you are spreading about the Catholic Church. My husband said you should be so ashamed to print such things about the true traditional church of God! How can you condemn God's church and His people? That is just one of the reasons I am leaving the Baptist church because of such back-biting, unreasonable, unlearned, unloving people that attend there that say they are believers in Christ. Marie, Internet

Response

We are all condemned because of sin. It is only when the gospel is proclaimed and believed that those condemned can be justified by God's sovereign grace. I pray you will obey the first command of Christ: "Repent and believe the gospel" (Mark 1:15).

Misinformed and Malicious

I recently came across your website and was depressed by what I saw. Your "service" is one of the most positively un-Christian, misinformed, and malicious services around. Shame on you! I pray for your darkened soul's conversion to the truth that now escapes you. Your mission cheapens Christianity and saddens me. L.V., Internet

Response

What cheapens Christianity is the ungodly practice of selling indulgences to accomplish that for which the Lord Jesus Christ shed His precious blood. May God penetrate your heart with the grace that will enable you to repent of this blasphemy.

Your Lack of Respect

I was shocked and horrified at your lack of respect for another of God's religions. Is there really such a strong need to degrade the Catholic Church in order to make your own faith sound more correct? Truly following in the steps of Jesus Christ requires the love of our fellow man. Did God mean for us to attack each other and continually put each other down only to develop our own personal status? Even the Scriptures in the Bible do not promote that sort of behavior. M. D., Plano, TX

Response

The Scriptures do indeed promote behavior that exposes, rebukes, and silences false teachers. We are exhorted to do this so that others will not be deceived (Titus 1:10–16). God abhors deceitful men (Psalm 5:6). No one should respect a religion that shuts the kingdom of heaven in men's faces (Matthew 23:13–14). It is not "love of our fellow man" to allow them to march proudly towards hell's gates without warning them. True love loves truth. "Better is open rebuke than love that is concealed" (Proverbs 27:5).

Your Hatred of Mary
Your web site is false and misleading. It is corrupt and misrepresents everything I know of the Catholic Church. Your hatred of Mary the mother of Christ is scary. Also, we have not rewritten the commandments as you claim. You must be so alone and scared to put in so much time defaming a Christian based religion. I am so sad for you. Your disgust for the Catholic faith permeates your website. Casey, Internet

Response
Sadly, it is your letter that is false and misleading. Nowhere on my website will you find my hatred of Mary. I love and respect her for her role as the mother of Jesus. The *New Catechism of the Catholic Church* (page 496) has indeed rewritten the Ten Commandments and purposefully left out the second one found in Exodus 20:2–17. The 2nd commandment forbids the making of graven images or statues in the likeness of anything in the heavens above or on the earth beneath or in the water below. It also forbids bowing down to them. My disgust for Roman Catholicism is because it has a death grip on my loved ones who are perishing with a false hope of sacramental salvation. I pray you will hear and understand the words of Christ and follow Him.

You Take the Word of God Too Seriously
You apparently believe and place all your belief in the Bible. The church or group you belong to is Bible-centered. The Catholic Church is not Bible-centered; it is Christ-centered. This may help you in the future to better understand a Catholic. Yours in Christ Jesus through mommy Mary, James, Internet

Response
By your own words you must go through Mary to get to Jesus, which is a reflection of your church's teaching. If you were Christ-centered you would recognize Jesus is the one mediator between God and man (1 Timothy 2:5). He is sufficient in His

— 216 —

mediation, His Word, His righteousness, His atonement, and His grace.

Witnessing to Catholics

I came across one of your tracts, "Scripture vs. Tradition." Two of our children are married to Catholic men and they don't want to hear anything about "our beliefs." I've tried many times to witness to them but to no avail. I would like all the help I can get in order to reach them for Christ. R.S., Wilkes Barre, PA

Response

When witnessing we must avoid sharing "our beliefs." The reason people are deceived is because they have believed someone else's beliefs rather than God's Word. When witnessing to Catholics it is best to use their Bible because they have been taught not to trust anything that is not Catholic. A good set of verses to walk them through is known as the Roman's Road (Romans 3:10; 3:23; 6:23; Revelation 20:14; Romans 5:8; 10:9–10). As they read each verse ask them what God is teaching them. This method allows God to speak powerfully and directly to them without your "beliefs" or interpretation, which they usually reject.

Your Attacks are Non-Christian

I've always been most respectful to other religions, including Jewish and Protestant. Your main target of attack and verbal destruction geared to the Catholic Church comes across as very non-Christian. I am very much offended by your mailings. May God forgive you and protect those souls who may in any way be affected or damaged by your deceitful messages. B.E. Miami, FL

Response

To respect people of another faith is commendable, but to respect religions that blind people from the truth of God's Word is deplorable. The wide road that leads to destruction is full of people who respect more than one way to salvation. Would you also call Jesus Christ "non-Christian" for His "verbal destruction" of the religious leaders of Israel (Matthew 23:13–36)? A Christian will gently correct those who are in opposition in hopes that God will grant them repentance leading to a knowledge of the truth (2 Timothy 2:25). I pray God will do that for you now. It is better to be offended with truth than perish living a lie.

Mother Teresa

I wonder what good can really come in evangelizing people away from the Catholic Church? I wonder what Mother Teresa would have said about your methods in discrediting the Catholic traditions, etc! I find her to be doing a lot more good in the world in comparison to your newsletter. M.C., Pardeeville, WI

Response

Since the official dogmas and teachings of the Catholic church oppose, veil, conceal, and distort the only means by which sinful man can be reconciled to our Holy God, it is of utmost importance that evangelicals point them to the narrow gate that leads to eternal life (Matthew 7:14). It should not matter to any true Christian what Mother Teresa (or any other human) would say since we are not to seek the approval of men, but God alone (Galatians 1:10). The Word of God calls us to expose the evil deeds of darkness (Ephesians 5:11), to hate every false way (Psalm 119:104), and to hate evil (Psalm 97:10). There is nothing more evil than deliberately withholding God's plan of salvation from those people destined for hell. Which is the greater good, to save people from their temporal problems of food, medicine, and shelter while ignoring their eternal problems, or to point people to Jesus, who is the only one who can save them from their eternal problem of sin and the lake of fire? While it is commendable that Mother Teresa helped the poor, she encouraged Buddhists to be better Buddhists and Hindus to be better Hindus. If she were convinced Jesus is the only way she might have pointed them to the Savior.

Catholic Ambiguity

I attended your seminar, "Roman Catholicism: Scripture vs Tradition" at Northwest Bible Church. Your zeal reminds me of the zeal with which Saul campaigned against the Christians. You tell what the Catholic Church says about itself by your quotes from its Catechism. However, you misrepresent it by taking passages out of context and leaving out important facts. You deliberately left out part of paragraph 2027 because it shows that Catholics really don't believe that we can merit or work our way to heaven as you claim that we do. Your misstatements of Catholic beliefs, backed up by Scripture verses, make the Catholic Church appear foolish. Mike, my prayer for you is that you will prayerfully, humbly, and sincerely study the teachings of the Catholic Church in their entirety and in context. Know what you really left. Please forgive us of any hurt or insensitivity we may have caused you as a Church. The door is always open for you. We've left the light on, too. M.H., Dallas, TX

Response

Many of the teachings in the Catechism are ambiguous. They attempt to be all things to all people, offering many roads to heaven except the only one God revealed in the Scriptures. Paragraph 2027 reads: "No one can merit the INITIAL grace which is at the origin of conversion. We can merit for ourselves and for others ALL the graces needed to attain eternal life." Which statement is one to believe? Paul makes it crystal clear that we cannot merit ANY grace (Romans 11:6). Another example of Catholic ambiguity regarding salvation is paragraph 841: "The plan of salvation also includes those who acknowledge the Creator, in the first place amongst whom are the Muslims." Are Catholics to believe this or paragraph 846, "they could not be saved who, knowing that the Catholic Church was founded as necessary by God through Christ, would refuse to enter it or to remain in it."

No Tolerance for Error

As a devout Catholic, I find your newsletter offensive to me. Your evangelizing efforts seem destructive at best. If you haven't noticed in our country, dialogue, cooperation, and plans are currently underway to bring the various faiths together with love and tolerance of our differences. Your intolerance will be judged, and by the very one you are proclaiming the gospel for! Your own flesh has misguided you. I study the same Bible you do, and for every misuse of holy scripture you proclaim to tear down His plan, you blaspheme the Holy Spirit. Truth is singular, and absolute, and mankind will never find his way alone. Our current post-Christian era will survive only through unity and love in Jesus Christ. C.D, Roswell, GA

Response

Jesus had no tolerance for anyone who opposed His teachings. He condemned the religious leaders of the first century for doing the very thing Catholic priests have been doing for centuries, shutting "the kingdom of heaven in men's faces" because of their spiritual blindness (Matthew 23:13–36). The Catholic clergy blocks the "narrow gate that leads to life" (Matthew 7:14) by denying that the perfect sacrifice of Christ is *finished* and *sufficient* to expiate and forgive the guilt and punishment of sin. It is only by trusting Christ and His Word that we will ever have true unity and love.

Assurance of Salvation

The Bible is quite clear that we are saved by faith, but faith alone cannot be enough. I know I am redeemed, and like Paul I am working out my salvation in fear and trembling (not self-confident assurance), with hopeful confidence—but not with a false assurance—and I do this as the Church has taught, unchanged, from the time of Christ. C.E., Louisville, KY

Response

If you believe you can lose your salvation you probably can. I know I cannot because I trust the One who promised to keep me from falling and present me blameless (Jude 24), the One who said no one (which includes me) can snatch me out of His hands (John 10:27–30). Paul is exhorting us to "work out" (that is, to exercise), not "work for" our salvation. If you believe the gospel you will trust the faithfulness and power of God to keep you, which is why eternal life is eternal and not temporal. Believe " The Promise" in 1 John 2:25.

Temporal Punishment

You claim that the concept of temporal punishment for sin in purgatory is as illogical as it is unbiblical. What does Paul mean by saying that Christians will barely be saved as if through fire? If the punishment for sin is death and Christ died on the cross for our sins, why do our bodies still suffer death? Frank, Internet

Response

All our works will be tested by fire. What is done for Christ, through Him (Galatians 2:20), will survive; whatever is left will be burnt up (I Corinthians 3:13–15). In this passage you will see it is the WORKS being tested by fire, NOT THE PERSON. There can be no temporal punishment for sin, since the wages of sin is death (Romans 6:23). Prior to Adam's sin, man was destined to live eternally both physically and spiritually with God. Sin entered into the world through Adam, and because of sin all men experience spiritual (Ezekiel 18:4) as well as physical death. That is why Christ said we must be born again to see the kingdom of God (John 3:3). Only through faith in Christ are we made spiritually alive (Ephesians 2:4). Those who reject Christ and His grace remain spiritually dead and separated from God's gracious presence. Those who are born once (physically) will die (physically and spiritually). Those who are born twice (physically and spiritually) will only die once (physically).

Christ is Immolated on Catholic Altars

I must correct your explanation of the Catholic Mass. The Church does NOT say that Christ is killed again at the altar. You have been lied to. The Church never taught this. This is calumny. Jesus is represented in an un-bloody sacrifice. It is the same sacrifice as Calvary, but Jesus is not killed. All your arguments are based on your (wrong) assumption that we Catholics keep killing Jesus. This is a lie. My positions are not my own, so to speak, because I submit my Biblical interpretations to the authority of the Church. You are your own authority. You answer to no one. Paul, Internet

Response

I would suggest that you are the one who has been lied to. According to the indisputable authority of the Catholic Church, Vatican Council II (page 102), it clearly states: "For in the sacrifice of the Mass Our Lord is immolated." According to Webster's Dictionary "immolate" means "to kill as a sacrificial victim." Those who read the Scripture know this is a lie because Paul wrote: "knowing that Christ, having been raised from the dead, is never to die again, death no longer is master over Him" (Romans 6:9). Be a good Berean and check the teachings of your church with Scripture to determine if they are true (Acts 17:11).

Faith Alone

Where in the Bible does it say you will be judged by your faith alone? I do not see any verse that says faith alone is all you will be judged on. Andy, Internet

Response

Let me point you to two verses that may help you. "To the one who *does not work, but believes* in Him who justifies the ungodly, his *faith* is reckoned as righteousness" (Romans 4:5). Jesus said, "He who hears My Word, and *believes* Him who sent Me, has eternal life and does not come into judgment" (John 5:24). So you see it is by faith and not by works that we are declared righteous, and therefore do not come under judgment for our sins. God judges sin either at the cross or at the final judgment. Those who have been saved by grace through faith and not by works had their sins judged and punished at Calvary (Ephesians 2:8–9). All who reject Christ and His substitutionary atonement will have their sins judged at the final judgment and will then be punished in the eternal lake of fire (Revelation 20:13–15). This includes all who deny the sufficiency of Christ's perfect sacrifice by believing their good works and sufferings can expiate their sins. Why would anyone refuse forgiveness and divine righteousness that is given freely to all who come to Christ with empty hands of faith?

Your Newsletter is Ridiculous

As a convert to Catholicism, I have heard that there are people who are very much against the Church; but not until your newsletter came to my address (unsolicited) had I ever read anything so ridiculous. The Devil is certainly alive and well for you to be spewing out such hatred. There surely are enough people for you to lead to Christ without your trying to "convert" Catholics. J.K., Carmel, IN

Response

Occasionally people send us names of their Catholic loved ones with the hope that they will read our newsletters and turn from the teachings and traditions of their church to the gospel of Christ and be saved. Tragically some of you choose to sever the lifeline to God's Word.

You are Uninformed about Scripture

It is obvious from what I read that you truly are uninformed when it comes to matters of Scripture. One thing that I have witnessed from all denominations that subscribe to the "Bible Alone Theory" is that they use only those pieces of Scripture that they want to read, and interpret them in amazing but misleading ways. The only thing they have in common is their disdain for the One,

Holy, Catholic, and Apostolic Church. Why do you feel that the Catholic Church teaches a gospel that includes additional requirements for salvation? I don't expect that either of us will "convert" the other. Mike, come on back. Steve, Internet

Response

The Bible gives overwhelming evidence as to why Scripture must be our sole authority for faith. The Word of God is holy, eternal, pure, perfect, inerrant, infallible, true, and forever settled in heaven (Psalm 19). It brings conviction, produces faith, and refutes error. Compare this with tradition. Jesus rebuked the religious leaders of His day for allowing their tradition to nullify the Word of God. Yet your church ignores this rebuke and elevates tradition above the authority of Scripture. Why would I return to a church that condemns me with over 100 anathemas for believing the gospel? Why would I return to a church that declares it is a sin if you believe that you are eternally secure in Christ? The *New Catechism of the Catholic Church* clearly teaches that sacraments, church membership, obeying the commandments, and good works are necessary for salvation. Furthermore, according to Vatican II, you must believe indulgences are efficacious for salvation or you are condemned with an anathema. As far as conversion is concerned, man cannot convert anyone. Conversion comes through the sanctifying work of the Spirit of God when one believes the Word of God (2 Thessalonians 2:13–14). My responsibility is to faithfully proclaim the gospel and pray the Holy Spirit convicts you of sin, righteousness, and the coming judgment (John 16:8–14).

Bigotry, Hate, and False Witness

Your material about Catholicism is mind-boggling! Why would you expend so much time and effort bearing false witness and promulgating bigotry and hate? Protestant reformation theology has successfully accomplished two things: (1) it has generated thousands of churches in disagreement about doctrine and hermeneutics, and (2) it has cultivated a stronger, more populous, more influential Catholic Church. Case in point: Over 500 years ago the sovereign heads of many nations were warring with the Catholic Church. Now the heads of those same nations do homage to the Pontiff of the Holy Roman Catholic Church. Consider Elizabeth I, who persecuted Catholics; now Elizabeth II curtsies to the Popes. Perhaps all Catholics should be thankful for the Reformation and it's aftermath because of the positive, strengthening influence it has had on Holy Mother Church. If you and your ilk successfully drew 150,000 Catholics a year away from the Church, what net effect is that? Over 200,000 Protestants converted to the Catholic Church in 2007 in the USA alone. Your work will never have any deleterious effect on the Church. Enjoy yourself. C.F., Internet

Response

It is not our work to draw away precious souls from a false religion; that is accomplished through the sanctifying work of the Holy Spirit as He applies the Word of God to their hearts (2 Thessalonians 2:13–14). Our work is to earnestly contend for the faith and to make disciples of Jesus Christ by faithfully proclaiming His gospel. As we do the work God has prepared for us, He will build His Church. Roman Catholicism has a large following because anyone can become a Catholic by the simple act of being sprinkled by a priest. On the other hand, no one can become a Christian unless the Father draws them to His Son and gives them the gift of faith (John 6:44, Ephesians 2:8–9). I pray you will turn from your popes and idols and seek God through His Word. "If you seek Him, He will let you find Him; but if you forsake Him, He will reject you forever" (1 Chronicles 28:9).

Proclaim the Gospel Where it is not Known

I was both alarmed and hurt by the video message on your website about the last days for Catholics. You misrepresented more than a few facts regarding the Catholic Church. I can appreciate your interest in attacking the church, but your time and energy would be better spent evangelizing in places where Christ is not yet known. As Catholics we believe that the only way to the Father is through the Son; and, if we are in error, you should not worry. You should be proclaiming the Good News where it is unknown and leave us to our Judge, the Sovereign Creator of all that is, was, and ever shall be. Gretchen S., Internet

Response

I pray the pain you felt from watching the video message will encourage you to examine yourself to make sure that your faith is in Christ alone. You are the one who should be "worried" about being in error. Those who embrace the false gospel of Catholicism are destined for the final judgment, where they will tremble with incredible fear as their sins are judged. There will be a prosecutor, but no defender, an indictment with no rebuttal, an unsympathetic judge with no jury, a verdict of guilty with no possibility of parole, an eternal sentence with no appeal into a prison with no possibility of escape. If you continue to reject the Savior by pursuing salvation through good works, indulgences, law keeping, and sacraments, this horrifying scene is what you can expect.

Catholic Funerals

A lifelong friend of mine passed away recently and, although I hate setting foot inside a Catholic church, I attended the funeral. This church was my parish for about 28 years, and I knew 90% of the people in attendance. When the priest began his sermon, I almost screamed. He explained, very dramatically, how we'll "all be together in heaven, whether you are a Muslim, Buddhist or Christian. God is called by different names–but He is the same God, and Jesus died so that all can go to heaven and be with God when we leave this life." I had known this was being taught, but it made me sick when I actually heard it. It breaks my heart to hear such blasphemy, but since he worships another Jesus and believes another gospel he is blinded to the truth. Have you ever tried to share the true gospel with a priest, face-to-face? I believe that the Lord is calling me to do just that, but I don't know how to approach him. I know that most evangelicals avoid confronting Catholic priests. What is your opinion? I am praying about this and asking God to lead me in whatever direction He wants me to go. S.P., Mount Juliet, TN

Response

What you described at the funeral is typical of the aberrant theology of Roman Catholic priests. We attended a funeral where the Catholic priest said, "We don't know where this man is (the deceased). He could be in a deep dark hole in outer space for all we know." Since priests do not know the truth they are tossed by every myth and wind of doctrine. I witness to priests as often as our Lord gives me divine appointments. I also witnessed to several Catholic bishops when they came to Dallas to discuss the sexual assault scandals of their priesthood. A good approach is to ask them to explain what Catholics must do to gain entrance into heaven. When they give the wrong answer, ask them this question: "If that is not true according to the Bible, would you want to know what God has revealed about this important issue?" I have yet to see any priest repent and believe the gospel, but we never know what God will do after the imperishable seeds of His Word are sown. I always leave a gospel tract behind and pray that God will use it to draw them to Himself. I encourage you to witness to priests and anyone and everyone else who is being held captive in religious deception.

Appendix 1

God's Amazing Grace
(In the life of Mike Gendron)

For many years I believed I was on the way to heaven, that is, until I began reading the Bible. I was horrified to see I was really destined for an eternity in hell. Being ignorant of God's word, I was following a way that seems right to a man, but in the end it leads to death (Proverbs 14:12). Then God called me to Himself through His gospel, which is the power of God for the salvation of everyone who believes (Romans 1:16). Now I know Jesus has saved me completely and forever! He has paid the complete punishment for all my sins and has given me the assurance of eternal life. Through His amazing grace, God has brought about some dramatic changes in my life. As a Roman Catholic for over 30 years, my life was characterized by four words–worldly, religious, enslaved and deceived. But thanks be to God, my life is now expressed, with heartfelt gratitude, by these four words–liberated, forgiven, reconciled and secured.

My Life Without Jesus

Worldly

From the world's perspective my first 34 years were uncommonly successful. I excelled in athletics, playing varsity baseball all the way through college, and winning a gold medal in springboard diving. After earning a master's degree in business, I channeled all my competitive energy into a rapid climb to the top of the corporate ladder. This enabled me to quickly obtain great wealth and recognition but it also led me into a hedonistic, pleasure-seeking lifestyle. I was corrupted by deceitful desires and had given myself over to sensuality, with a continual lust for more (Ephesians 4:19). I built my half million-dollar dream house in one of the most prestigious neighborhoods in Dallas, joined a fabulous country club, purchased a Mercedes 380 SL sports car, and (the universal sign of accomplishment) a gold Rolex watch. Yet with all this success and wealth, there was still a nagging void in my life. "For all that is in the world, the lust of the flesh and the lust of the eyes and the boastful pride of life, is not from God, but is from the world" (1 John 2:16).

Enslaved

My enslavement was all encompassing and I was powerless to do anything about it. Not only was I in bondage to sin, but also to the legalism of Catholic traditions (Colossians 2:8). The Catholic priests, like the Judaizers, were false brethren who kept me in bondage (Galatians 2:4). Their confessional box was a place I dreaded to go. Each week I had to confess the same sins to the same priest because I was "disobedient, deceived, and enslaved to various lusts and pleasures" (Titus 3:3). Many times I would disguise my voice so the priest wouldn't know that it was me again. Undeniably, I was "ensnared by the devil, held captive by him to do his will" (2 Timothy 2:26).

Religious

As a devout Catholic, I faithfully participated in religious rituals and received the sacraments to merit God's grace and to avoid the fires of hell. In retrospect I was motivated more by a fear of hell than a desire to be with God. Some of my good works included being an altar boy for 7 years, teaching Catholic doctrine to high school students, and initiating the first Little Rock Scripture Study at a Catholic Church in Dallas. This religious activity gave me an external righteousness that covered my corrupt and depraved nature. Yet according to Isaiah, all my righteous acts were like filthy rags (64:6). I had a zeal for God but it wasn't based on biblical knowledge so I sought to establish my own righteousness before God (Romans 10:1). Now I know how Satan destroys religious people for their lack of knowledge (Hosea 4:6).

Deceived

I had no way to discern truth from error because I was biblically ignorant. It wasn't that I didn't have a Bible; in fact, I had a huge one displayed in my home as a sign of piety. I never bothered to read it because the priests told me it was too difficult to understand. No one ever told me the Bible sets forth the truth plainly to every man's conscience (2 Corinthians 4:2). Because of my lack of biblical knowledge I was easily deceived. I lived in error because I did not know the Scriptures or the power of God (Matthew 22:29). Satan, who deceives the whole world, had blinded me from the truth of the gospel (Revelation 12:9; 2 Corinthians 4:4). I was separated from the life of God because of the ignorance that was in me (Ephesians 4:18).

My Life With Jesus

Liberated

In 1981, after attending an apologetics seminar called "Evidence for the Christian Faith," the Bible became my sole authority in all matters of faith. I began searching for answers to questions that priests were unable to explain. I was amazed at how often the Bible contradicted Catholic teaching and tradition. Soon I faced a difficult dilemma. With my eternal destiny hanging in the balance I had to make a decision. Should I trust the Word of God or the teachings and traditions of the Catholic Church? Once I saw it from that perspective it became an easy decision. The truth of God's Word began to set me free from the legalistic bondage of the Catholic Church. I read where Jesus came to release the captives, and to set free those who are downtrodden (Luke 4:18). He said, "If you abide in My Word, then you are truly disciples of Mine; and you shall know the truth, and the truth shall make you free" (John 8:31–32). The ransom payment for delivering sinners from the bondage of sin was the precious blood of Jesus. He "gave Himself for us, that He might redeem us from every lawless deed, and purify for Himself a people for His own possession, zealous for good deeds" (Titus 2:14). It is through the indwelling power of the Holy Spirit that I can put to death the evil deeds of the flesh (Romans 8:13). The battle between my sin nature and the indwelling Holy Spirit is ever present within me, but by God's grace sin no longer is master over me. Sin remains, yes, but it does not reign. Thanks be to God that, though I was a slave of sin, by His power He made me a slave of righteousness (Romans 6:17–18).

Forgiven

As a Catholic, each time I confessed my sins to a priest he told me I was forgiven. But was I really? I never even knew what God's forgiveness meant or what God's justice demanded as punishment for sin. Each time I entered the Catholic Church I saw Jesus hanging on a cross, but I never knew why he had to die. I never knew, that is, until I read in the Bible that the penalty for sin is death, eternal separation from God in the lake of fire (Romans 6:23, Revelation 20:14). The debt that must be paid to satisfy God's justice, and His anger over sin, is death. Then I discovered "to forgive" means "to cancel a debt that is owed." So when God forgives a sinner He cancels the entire debt for all their sins—past, present and future. My substitute, Jesus Christ cancelled the certificate of debt against me. It was nailed to the cross (Colossians 2:14). Jesus suffered and died so that I could live. He was pierced for my transgressions. He was crushed for my iniquities (Isaiah 53:5). Oh, how can it be that my God and Creator should die for me? The answer is profoundly given in one word—love. "God demonstrated His own love toward us in that while we were yet sinners, Christ died for us" (Romans 5:8). My sin, not in part but the whole, was nailed to the cross. I bear it no more! God made Him who knew no sin to be sin on my behalf, so that I might become the righteousness of God in Him (2 Corinthians 5:21). This was the greatest news I had ever heard! No longer was I condemned to death, but justified to life! I was acquitted because God, the righteous Judge, saw that justice was served through His Only Son. "Jesus abolished death and brought life and immortality to light through the gospel" (2 Timothy 1:10) "Through His name everyone who believes in Him receives forgiveness of sins" (Acts 10:43).

Reconciled

Once I knew I had been reconciled to God through the death of His Son, I no longer needed priests offering sacrifices for my sins. "For by one offering Jesus has perfected for all time those who are sanctified" (Hebrews 10:14). No longer is there a sin barrier separating me from God (Isaiah 59:2). Jesus has given me access to the Father (Ephesians 2:18). This was powerfully demonstrated at His death when the four-inch temple veil, separating man and his sin from God, was torn open from top to bottom. "Christ died for sins once for all, the just for the unjust, in order that He might bring us to God" (1 Peter 3:18). Those who trust the redeeming work of Christ can exchange their religion for a relationship with almighty God. Through the blood of His cross Jesus is able to present me before God holy and blameless (Colossians 1:20–22). Jesus changed my relationship with God from one of hostility to one of peace and harmony.

Secured

When I was a Roman Catholic, each time I got on an airplane I experienced a nagging fear as to where I would spend eternity if the plane went down. I never knew if my sins were serious enough to warrant hell or if I had done enough good works to qualify for heaven. Now, as a Christian, I know eternal life is not determined by what I do for God, but by what God has done for me. I no longer have to wonder about my eternal destiny. It is based on the assertive faithfulness of God. I am secure in Christ and nothing I do will ever change God's promises to me. Jesus promised that He will lose no one the Father has given Him. "For this is the will of My Father, that everyone who beholds the Son and believes in Him may have eternal life; and I Myself will raise him up on the last day" (John 6:39–40). I came to realize that eternal life, by its very nature, can never be terminated. I am held securely in the hands of the Father and the Son and no one can snatch me away (John 10:27–30). Those whom God justifies He also glorifies (Romans 8:30). "The Holy Spirit, who is given as a pledge of our inheritance, seals everyone who hears and believes the gospel of salvation in Christ" (Ephesians 1:13-14). Based on God's promises, I am more confident of spending eternity in heaven than one more day on earth.

I am forever thankful that God has made me alive in Christ, healed my spiritual blindness, adopted me into His family, and given me the privilege of telling others about His amazing grace! The life I live I now live for Him!

Resources

Proclaiming the Gospel Ministry offers a variety of books, audio CDs, video messages on DVDs, tracts and booklets to help you grow in the grace and knowledge of our Lord Jesus Christ and discern truth from error. These tools will also help you become an effective witness for Jesus Christ.

Tracts & Booklets

Roman Catholicism: Scripture vs. Tradition

A four-color, 16-panel tract that shows how the new *Catechism of the Catholic Church* opposes and contradicts the official New American-Catholic Bible on the most critical issues relating to the Gospel of Jesus Christ. The tract gives a brief history of the Catholic Church, a doctrinal timeline, a glossary of Catholic terms, as well as contrasting doctrines of Jesus, His work of redemption, salvation, the gospel, and the path to eternity. This tract was developed to persuade Catholics to trust the infallible Word of God as their ultimate authority for truth instead of the teachings and traditions of men.

Have You Ever Been Deceived?

The nature of deception is such that no one knows they are deceived until they are lovingly confronted with the truth. This tract is a compassionate plea for those who are lost in religion to examine the object of their faith and their source for truth. A persuasive argument is given to trust God's Word instead of man's teachings and traditions.

Rome vs. The Bible

This tract shows eleven distinctive ways the core beliefs of Roman Catholics and Christians are contradictory. This is a timely tract, considering the strong push for ecumenical unity between evangelicals and Catholics. This tract will show evangelicals why there can never be unity with Catholics and why the Roman Catholic religion represents the largest and most neglected mission field in the world.

The Greatest News

This six-page tract presents the plan of salvation using only the power of God's Word. It is a provocative outline that reveals six key elements of the glorious gospel of grace: God's Perfection, Man's Problem, God's Provision, Man's Part, God's Promise, and Man's Privilege.

Which Jesus Do You Trust?

A thought-provoking contrast between the Eucharistic Jesus and the Jesus of Scripture is presented using Scripture and the Catholic Catechism. The precious souls who are embracing a counterfeit Christ must be lovingly warned. This tract is also available in Spanish.

True Faith or False Hope - How Can I Be Sure?

An excellent tract that will challenge professing Christians who have shown very little, or no, evidence of being born again. The Gospel tract encourages people to test themselves to see if they have genuine faith. (2 Corinthians 13:5).The most terrifying words a professing Christian could ever hear on judgment day would be these words of Jesus: "I never knew you; depart from me, you workers of lawlessness" (Matthew 7:23). Jesus said those horrifying words will be heard, not by a few, but by many who called Him "Lord" but never repented of their iniquities.

Gospel Cards.

Twelve beautifully illustrated, full color cards that make the Gospel clear and complete according to Scripture.

Video Messages on DVD

Accompanied by PowerPoint/Keynote Slides

Mystery Spiritual Babylon

She is described as a world-wide religious system with roots in Babylon where all false religions were spawned by seducing spirits and doctrines of demons. You must decide if there is enough evidence to convict Roman Catholicism as the woman holding the golden cup full of abominations.

Catholicism's Drift into Apostasy

While Roman Catholicism claims to be the one-true church founded by Christ, she has a sordid history of corruption and apostasy. This message reveals how the Roman Catholic Church officially and dogmatically departed from the faith of the apostles at the Council of Trent in the 16th century.

False Converts in the Church

The most terrifying words any professing Christian could ever hear would be Jesus Christ declaring, "I never knew you, depart from Me." This message exhorts Christians and their loved ones to examine their faith with the Word of God.

Evangelicals and Catholics: Reversing the Reformation.

Many evangelicals continue to sign unity accords with Catholics in spite of the differences that sparked the Reformation.

Which Gospel?

God's gospel is under attack in three critical areas: (1) the Christ of the gospel, (2) the promises of the gospel, and (3) the response to the gospel.

Rescuing Loved Ones from God's Wrath.
God's Word exhorts Christians to save others, snatching them out of the fire (Jude 23). If we could get a brief glimpse of the terrifying wrath of a just God being poured out on sinners, we would do everything possible to bring our loved ones to the Savior.

Why Should Anyone Believe the Bible?
Ten verifiable claims that show the Bible is the most unique and supernatural book ever written.

Prophecy and the Pope
Reveals predictions of Catholic "saints" and mystics who say the papacy will convert the world to Catholicism and a Catholic monarch will rule the people.

The Death of Discernment
We must learn how to discern God's truth from the error of religious leaders to avoid being swept away by every wind of doctrine.

The Best Kept Secret in the Church
Many Christians live without peace and assurance because they have never heard or understood this key doctrine in John's first epistle.

Identifying and Opposing False Teachers
Learn how to identify deceivers and expose their lies with God's truth.

Why Evangelize if God Has Already Chosen?
See how divine sovereignty and human responsibility work together in God's perfect plan of redemption.

The Coming One-World Religion
Reveals prophecies describing the formation of Satan's global religion. Catalysts for ecumenical unity and the strategic role of the Vatican are examined.

Tell Catholics the Truth

Explains why we must tell Catholics that there is only one supreme objective authority that can be trusted, the inspired Word of God.

Satan's Attacks on the Christian Faith

Reveals how the devil's legions of liars are assaulting the supremacy of God's Word, the sufficiency of God's Son, the singularity of God's gospel, the sovereignty of God's grace, the security of God's children, and the sanctity of God's church.

Are You Sure You Are a Christian?

Tragically, there are many who profess Christ who have never been born again. Test yourselves to see if you are in the faith (2 Corinthians 13:5).

Jesus Christ vs. Antichrist

Reveals a compelling contrast between two Christs. There are many who will be deceived by the Antichrist because they do not know the true Christ.

Which Jesus Do You Trust?

A convincing contrast between the Jesus of Roman Catholicism and the Jesus of Scripture.

The Bible-Driven Church

Looks at the Biblical characteristics of the true church contrasted with the marks of the post-modern emerging church.

Deception and Apostasy

Explores the growing apostasy within the church and identifies some of its causes.

Hard Questions for Good Catholics

Asking questions is a highly effective method of evangelism, and was often used by the Lord Jesus Christ in His encounters with people blinded by religious traditions. He asked challenging and thought-provoking questions of the Jews to expose the errors of their teachings. This message offers the same kind of questions that can be asked of Catholics who embrace the traditions of men instead of the Word of God.

Last Days for Catholics

God does not promise anyone tomorrow; today is the day of salvation. The gospel must be proclaimed with a growing sense of urgency. This important message looks at Roman Catholicism through the lens of Scripture. By denying the supreme authority of God's Word and the sufficiency of Jesus Christ, Catholics have created another gospel that has no power to save souls.

Roman Catholicism vs. Evangelical Christianity

Dr. David Reagan interviews Mike Gendron with sensitivity and compassion as they explore how Catholics have been led to trust a different authority, believe another gospel, and worship another Christ.

To order resources contact:

Proclaiming the Gospel Ministry
2829 Veranda Lane
Southlake, TX 76092

Or you may order through our award winning web site:

www.ProclaimingTheGospel.org